THE CONCEPT OF HOLINESS

O. R. JONES

THE CONCEPT
OF
HOLINESS

LONDON
GEORGE ALLEN & UNWIN LTD
RUSKIN HOUSE MUSEUM STREET

FIRST PUBLISHED IN 1961

PRINTED IN GREAT BRITAIN
in 11 pt. Pilgrim type
BY EAST MIDLAND PRINTING CO. LTD.
BURY ST. EDMUNDS

ACKNOWLEDGEMENTS

I am deeply indebted to Professor I. T. Ramsey, Oriel College, Oxford for his painstaking interest in this work which would never have appeared in its present form but for his valuable criticisms, his many constructive suggestions and his constant encouragement. Professor R. I. Aaron, University College of Wales, Aberystwyth read the whole typescript, while Dr D. A. Rees, Jesus College, Oxford and Mr H. S. Eveling, University of Edinburgh read parts of it, and all have made many worthwhile suggestions which I have utilized and for which I am very grateful. Professor Aaron and Dr D. O. Thomas, University College of Wales, Aberystwyth, kindly read the proofs. I also take this opportunity of thanking my former teachers at Bangor, Professor H. D. Lewis, now of King's College, London and Mr T. H. McPherson, for all that I have learnt from them about the philosophy of religion.

Aberystwyth
June 1961

CONTENTS

CHAPTER I

INTRODUCTION

No serious religious thinker can afford to ignore the changes that have come about in the philosophical scene in Britain during the past two or three decades, for there can be no doubt that those changes have precipitated special problems for religious thought. A few such problems have already been raised, often in a general way, and discussed by philosophers who have not only a religious interest but who are also acutely aware of the changes to which I refer. There is no need to recapitulate here what they have said since it is readily available for the careful reading which it deserves. It will be a sufficient indication of the kind of discussion I have in mind if I mention for example: the volume edited by Alasdair MacIntyre and A. G. N. Flew published under the title *New Essays in Philosophical Theology, Christianity and Paradox* by R. W. Hepburn, and *Faith and Logic*, edited by Basil Mitchell, a book in which the general theistic problem is stated very clearly by I. M. Crombie.

One very important point that emerges from these discussions is that religious concepts are very different from the concepts that enter into everyday discourse and into high-level discussions within the fields of science, politics and aesthetics. One could insist, as many have done, that religious concepts can only be treated as belonging to one or other of these spheres, and then proceed to argue that religious language comprises some false statements, many empty or meaningless sentences, a considerable body of moral pronouncements, and a host of emotional expressions. I, for one, am not convinced that nothing important is missed by treating religious language in this way, and would rather plead for a recognition of its oddity. Here is a field of discourse which is unlike any other and which calls for an open-minded approach if it is to be correctly mapped out. This is not to say that religious discourse is *totally* unlike any other, and that there is no connection whatsoever between this particular kind of discourse and others. Thus we cannot afford to turn our backs completely on ordinary language, for whatever the last word is, here as elsewhere the *first* word *is* ordinary language—a point which J. L. Austin so aptly made in another context.[1] What we must avoid is to approach religious language with some definite preconceptions about its general nature. So let it be recognized at the start that religious language is odd, strange, difficult and often baffling.

How can such a field of discourse be illuminated? Since we cannot begin with generalizations about the placing of religious language with respect to scientific or any other language, the plausible alternative is surely to begin with particular religious concepts and work at our task piecemeal.[2] If our investigation into the logic of particular concepts does eventually throw up some more general suggestions then well and good, but it seems to me that much work requires to be done at the more particular level first. That is why I have chosen to centre my enquiry in this book upon one particular religious concept. My investigation throws up one rather general suggestion at a fairly early stage, and this suggestion is given more prominence as the enquiry proceeds. Towards the end of the book I consider at some length a key-concept which I suspect is a central knot with which most, if not all, other religious concepts have a direct or indirect tie, though my main interest here will naturally be in its ties with the concept which I have initially chosen for investigation, namely, the concept of holiness.

My only reason for choosing this particular concept is that it appears to be more purely religious than others such as creation, love, and so forth—concepts which have obvious analogies in everyday language. If my assumption has anything in it, then I would expect an investigation of the concept of holiness to take us nearer to the heart of what is distinctive in religious discourse, and to do this reasonably soon. The topic is of course a very large one, but I have set myself limits by confining the discussion to the sphere of Hebrew and Christian belief and practice. Whatever is to be said eventually about the

---

[1] *Proceedings of the Aristotelian Society* New Series Vol. LVII p. 11.
[2] Cf. a point made by Professor Austin in the above-mentioned paper.

concept in view of its spread through many different religions we need to study first the role it plays in each particular religion.

A peculiar difficulty attends the task I have set myself, for it requires that justice be done to two very different disciplines. One must try to meet, and satisfy, both the theologian and the philosopher. On those occasions when both sides have met in recent years the general feeling has been that they were failing to secure engagement with each other in discussion. The theologian finds it difficult to grasp what some present-day philosophers are about, while the philosophers themselves tend to take religious utterances at their face value and are mystified when the theologians insist that they are not to be understood in that way. If one is to make any contribution towards the bridging of this gulf then the philosophical questions must be understood, borne in mind, and met, but also religious concepts must be fairly dealt with by looking carefully into their background connections in religious belief and practice. The result of an attempt to do both these things may well be that members of the philosophical camp will feel that philosophical rigour has been abandoned and that the book is addressed to theologians only, while the theologians themselves may well fail to see why so much time should be lost following up a grammatical clue and discussing the ordinary everyday use of certain words. This is, perhaps, inevitable until the two sides discover a common ground.

A thorough research into the relevant literature of theism is certainly necessary if one is to give fair consideration to any religious concept, and the philosopher needs to be constantly reminded of the importance of this rather unphilosophical preliminary investigation. With regard to the concept of holiness the amount of relevant literature is vast even when the investigation is confined to Hebrew and Christian literature, but on close examination one is soon struck by the fact that there are a few main associate notions such as that of fear, power, and others, which help the explorer to find his bearings. It is in terms of such associate notions that I have found it possible to organize the relevant material and display the role played by holiness in Hebrew and Christian religious literature. Furthermore, these associate notions serve as transition points between that aspect of my inquiry in which I deal with Hebrew and Christian literature on the one hand, and on the other, that in which I deal with the logic of 'holiness'. For instance, once it is realized that holiness is often thought of as being a 'power' of some kind we can, firstly, concentrate our attention on the use of this word in ordinary everyday situations, and then proceed further to consider its exceptional use in connection with holiness. What is true of the notion of power goes for the other associated notions as well. Such words as 'fearful', 'power', 'separatedness', 'wholeness', and 'goodness' may seem capable of acting as substitutes for 'holiness' in certain contexts, and those are the contexts which will require close scrutiny. But it will emerge that, though these words in religious contexts are logically very similar to the word 'holiness' itself, yet they do not fill its place adequately. When 'power' is mentioned in connection with holiness the implications of the word 'power' will extend beyond those of its everyday use, yet it will not be entirely divorced from its everyday use either. The word 'power' (and this goes for the other comparable words that I have mentioned) has an ordinary everyday use, but has also been used in an exceptional way in religious contexts, and my intention is to throw some light on the concept of 'holiness' by looking fairly closely at these contexts.

The various fields of discussion are then integrated by the introduction of one key-concept which promises to help us to understand what is exceptional about the holy situation in each case—where holiness is an exceptional object of fear, an exceptional power, an exceptional kind of goodness and so forth. This key-concept is 'divine personality', a suggestion which arises from seeing that the holy situation is always 'personal' in an exceptional sense.

I am well aware of the sketchy nature of my discussion of the all-important key concept, that is, 'divine personality'. A whole host of unanswered questions cluster around several of the points that are made, but it seems to me that a thorough consideration of each of these would take one far beyond the limits of one book. Meanwhile I may perhaps claim that at least some progress has been made with the task of illuminating the concept of holiness in so far as it is shown that the concepts 'fear', 'power', 'love', 'wholeness', and 'goodness', when associated with 'holiness' also have special links with the concept 'divine personality', I have pressed on regardless of a host of problems in order to present a general picture of what our talk about holiness involves. It is, perhaps, some small contribution to have shown how the study of a religious concept can involve, and bring us up against, a rich nexus of questions which have by no means been disposed of in philosophy. It is so easy to do otherwise, to give religious concepts rough and peremptory treatment, and to adopt a categorical and reductive method which can miss so much and make the philosophy of religion appear a dead subject.

CHAPTER II

IS HOLINESS A QUALITY?

To what extent can the logic of 'holiness' be assimilated to that of grammatical kinsmen such as 'whiteness', 'loudness', 'hardness', and 'sweetness'? Not that grammar is by any means an infallible guide to logic, and to suppose so would be to ignore a constant and important theme of contemporary philosophy.[1] But there is more than grammatical likeness which suggests that holiness is a quality. Holiness is predicated of many very different things; there are holy places, there is at least one holy book, and bread, water, and vestments, despite their obvious diversity, are all called holy. Is there anything else that we can predicate of such a variety of objects? We immediately think of a common characteristic such as colour for example; whiteness can be predicated of a wide variety of things such as paper, snow, clouds, skin, clothes, flowers and so forth. There seems to be a parallel here which further justifies us in going on to compare quality words like 'whiteness' or 'greyness' with 'holiness'. It might be thought that the latter is a quality which various different objects have in common.

Now all the words which I have brought alongside the word 'holiness' refer more or less directly to something which can be perceived by sense-experience. Whiteness is exemplified by the particular colour seen when we perceive anything that is white, loudness has to do with the particular intensity of an audible sound, hardness with the feel of an object when touched, and sweetness with the taste of various edibles. These particular data of sense-experience were classed together by the British Empiricists (such as Locke) as 'ideas', and by Russell as 'sense-data'; they might be generally referred to as qualities of objects. Caution should, however, be exercised in the grouping together

[1] See B. Russell in *Mysticism and Logic* Ch. X (Longmans, 1918) and Susan Stebbing in *Modern Introduction to Logic* Ch. IX (Methuen, 1945) and later G. Ryle in 'Systematically misleading expressions', which appears in *Logic and Language (First Series)* Ch. II, (Ed. A. G. N. Flew, Blackwell, 1953).

of such terms. It is so easy to cloud the differences between, for example, 'loudness' and 'greyness' and treat them as though their logical behaviour was exactly the same in all respects. Plainly this is not so, for 'greyness' refers to a *kind* of colour whereas 'loudness' does not refer to a kind of sound but to its *intensity*. Thus 'loudness' is logically more akin to the word 'brightness' than to 'greyness'. However, I wish to leave any questions concerning such differences quite open, for my immediate interest is in what is common to all the words in my list, namely that they all refer to something which can be perceived by sense experience. Whatever the differences and similarities between 'loudness', 'brightness' and 'greyness', they all involve a reference to something that is objective in a perceptual situation, what we hear in the case of the first word, and what we see in the case of the other two.

The question that now arises is: is an instance of holiness something which we perceive through sense-experience? Supposing we were asked to state whether holiness was visible or audible, or whether it was a taste, a smell or a 'feel', how should we answer? No straightforward answer springs readily to mind. There does not seem to be a particular colour called 'holy' any more than there is a sound, a smell, taste or a 'feel' which exemplifies 'holiness'. What perceptible factor could there be which was common to water, vestments, churches, persons and even days and ceremonies, all of which can be holy? There seems to be nothing definite in all instances for which we should look or listen, which we should touch, taste, or smell in order to decide whether or not anything is holy. Some people use this fact as one of their premises for arguing that holiness means nothing at all. With reference to water that is called holy they will ask: what is the difference between this water and any other? They presuppose that holiness must refer to something perceptible if it is to mean anything at all, and they know that the devout worshipper is unwilling, and they suspect that he is unable, to mention anything of the kind, so they hope to force him to give up his claim that any water is holy, or to admit that it is a pointless claim. So long as it is assumed that 'holiness' must be like such words as 'greyness', 'loudness' and so forth, in having a reference to something that

B   17

can be perceived by sense-experience, the claims of the sacra-
mentalist seem to have little or no force.

There are other factors too which tell against bundling the
word 'holiness' into the same logical group as these others. It is
for example appropriate to ask for a scientific explanation for a
thing being a certain colour, having certain smells and tastes,
for sound having various forms and intensities. Colour
differentiation can be explained in terms of light-waves which
vary in length, and hardness can be explained by referring to
different density of molecules in various materials, and comparable explanations can be expected for smells and tastes and
sounds. It may be questionable whether science gives us all the
explanations we could have, and I do not wish to enter into
that here. My point is that scientific explanation is relevant in
the case of colours, sounds, tastes, 'feels', and smells in a way
in which it is not relevant in the case of holiness. One would
not ask for a scientific explanation for holiness as one would
ask for such an explanation of a sense-impression. It must of
course be granted that some holy waters are believed to have
healing powers, and then scientific explanation might come
into the picture at some point or other. Even in this case, however, the scientist would not be concerned to explain why the
waters were holy, but rather to understand why they had
healing effects. If such waters are regarded as holy because of
their healing power, then that is a different matter. We shall
see later that the Hebrews did indeed react to holiness as though
it was a power, though it could be destructive as well as life-
giving in its effects. What I want to emphasize at the moment,
however, is that holiness is not something which makes an
impression on any of our five senses in a way that makes it
appropriate to ask for a scientific explanation for the source of
that impression. And in this respect it is very different from
greyness, hardness, sweetness and so forth.

There is yet another aspect of this difference between 'holiness' and these other words which I have mentioned. They all
refer to something which can only be appreciated through a
specific organic part of the body. Whiteness can only be properly appreciated by seeing white things with our eyes, loudness is gauged by hearing with our ears. It is by touching,

tasting, or sniffing that we find out whether anything is hard, bitter, or perfumed. But there is no particular sense or sense-organ that has been traditionally associated with the experience or appreciation of holiness. We feel quite sure that inability to see debars us from appreciating whiteness, that inability to taste debars us from appreciating sweetness, and so forth, but there is no specific sense the cutting off of which would be considered detrimental to our appreciation of holiness.

Further, if I claim to know that a thing is white, there are certain tests and checks that can be made to prove or disprove my contention. Other people could look at the object in question, its surface could be scientifically compared with others, light-waves could be measured, and photographs could be taken. None of these checks would be relevant to the claim that a place, thing or person is holy. Holy water is not tested by giving it to other people to taste, or by subjecting it to chemical analysis. Even if 'radio-activeness' were coined as a word in our language, 'holiness' would not be like that either. Though radio-activeness could not be directly sensed if its concentration was very small, there would still be some tests and checks which depended in the last resort upon sense-experience to which appeal could be made. But there is no accepted scientific method of testing for holiness. Holiness is not even indirectly, or at the second move, scientifically testable. There may indeed be a few people who want to claim that holiness is testable by radiaesthesia. Some have claimed that holy water, for example, should produce a cross on a certain sensitive plate. Such claims however have not been substantiated to such a degree as to merit much serious consideration. In any case the large majority of religious believers do not wish to make such claims, and this implies that they do not think of holiness as being the sort of thing that could be tested in that way at all.

Enough has now been said to suggest that the word 'holiness' simply will not be cajolled into the same logical group as 'greyness', 'loudness', 'sweetness', and 'hardness', and the upshot of this seems to be that holiness is not the same sort of thing as greyness, loudness, sweetness or hardness. But there is also another side to the picture. I now want to put this by examining an argument which, despite what I have just said, holds that there is an analogy between knowing a colour and knowing holiness. It might be argued that though holiness is different from colours, sounds, tastes and smells in the various ways I have mentioned, yet it is like them in that it is also known directly, and non-inferentially. While it is admitted in this argument that holiness is not the sort of thing that can be seen or heard in the ordinary sense of those words, it is maintained that we have an awareness of holiness which is just as direct and non-inferential as, for example, seeing a particular colour x without seeing *that* it is x. This view is held by H. H. Farmer in the book *Towards Belief in God* where he says that we must assume that 'the capacity to become aware of God is part of normal human nature *like the capacity to see light or to hear sound*'.[2] John Baillie holds a rather similar view in his book *Our Knowledge of God* where he says that our knowledge of God is like 'our knowledge of tridimensional space and all other primary modes of knowledge, something that cannot be imagined by one who does not already possess it, since it cannot be described to him in terms of anything else than itself'.[3] Otto's contention, that the mental state which is associated with the objective 'numinous' is *sui generis*, lends itself to a similar interpretation. Of the numinous Otto says, 'little of it can usually be noticed in theory and dogma, or even in exhortation, unless it is actually *heard*'.[4] What is there in this assimilation of an awareness of holiness to sense-experience? What can we make of this claim for immediate awareness?

Let us consider the matter in the light of a distinction that can be drawn between two different senses of the word 'see'. In saying 'the bull sees red' I could be using the word 'see' to refer primarily to the bull's experience. In that case it is not assumed that the bull recognizes the colour in question as red. He does not know that it is called 'red' in English, and he does not necessarily know that it it the same colour as he saw the day before yesterday. The bull presumably reacts without knowing *that* anything is the case when he charges at the unfortunate boy wearing a red jersey. At any rate, we do not

[2] *Towards Belief in God* p. 40 (italics mine) (S.C.M. Press, 1942).
[3] *Our Knowledge of God* p. 217 (Oxford, 1939).
[4] *The Idea of the Holy* p. 65 (italics mine) (Oxford, 1936).

usually intend to imply that the bull has *understood* anything when we say that he has seen red—not even that he has recognized the colour as a certain shade of red or as distinct from any other colour. He might have been a blind bull who had just got his sight a moment ago when the first and only colour he saw was this particular shade of red. Of course *we* express what we suppose that he experiences by saying that he 'sees red'. It is true that the best way of expressing in English one's experience of seeing red would be to use the words 'I see red', and that use would presuppose that we *recognized* red and knew how to use the word 'red' and so forth. We could however have the experience of seeing red without ever saying anything about it; I chose the example of the bull seeing red precisely because bulls do not tell us what they have seen. It is to 'seeing' in this sense of the word, that is where we would distinguish it from seeing *that* something is the case, that we usually refer when we talk of 'sensation'.

I now come to a different sense of the word 'see'. Consider the circumstances in which someone might say 'I see now what the figure represents—it is a duck'.[5] The person in question may have been looking at this particular figure for quite a time before he sees it as a duck. He might have been seeing it as a rabbit's head the whole time, or maybe he could not see anything more than a few meaningless lines on a piece of paper. In the first sense of the word 'see' which I have distinguished, he had seen everything from the start. When he did 'see' the figure as a duck then he did not see any more hitherto undiscovered lines or dots. In the first sense of the word 'see' he sees no more at the end than he did at the beginning. When, after staring with puzzlement at the figure for some time, the person says, 'Oh! I see, it is a duck', then he is using the word 'see' in a special sense. To see in this second sense of the word is to grasp a pattern which had been missed in the first place, and the apprehension of this pattern involves grasping a whole complex of facts together. It is to see that a certain projection in the drawing is a beak and that the little circle is an eye, and so forth. This seeing is an intellectual matter—we might call

[5] This example comes from Wittgenstein's *Philosophical Investigations* p. 194 (Blackwell, 1953) though my present point is not precisely the same as his.

it intellectual discernment to distinguish it from the first kind of seeing which is pure sensation. As 'seeing' in the first sense is connected with eyesight, so 'seeing' in this last sense is connected with intellectual ability. I shall say more about this 'seeing' at a much later stage in my discussion; I have said enough for the moment to distinguish it from the first kind of 'seeing' which I mentioned. In order to avoid confusion, I shall use the word 'sensation' to refer to the first kind of 'seeing' and the term 'intellectual discernment' when I wish to refer to 'seeing' in the second sense.

Though sensation and intellectual discernment are to be clearly distinguished yet there is a close parallel between them in our experience. This is indicated by the fact that words which are appropriate in the context of sensation also find a use in the context of intellectual discernment as well. Not only is the word 'see' itself common to both realms, but such phrases as 'it *dawned* on me', 'it is *clear* to me now', 'so and so threw *light* on my problem', are used of intellectual discernment as well as of sensation. Since there is this close connection between the two types of 'seeing' in our experience, it is not surprising to find that a few words have acquired an ambiguous use in which it is not clear whether they relate to 'seeing' in the one sense or the other. 'Awareness' and 'knowledge' are such terms. When Farmer speaks of a 'capacity to become aware of God' does he consider 'becoming aware of' to be very much like 'seeing' in the first or the second of the above-mentioned senses? The context seems to me to weigh in favour of the first sense, for he adds that it is like the capacity to '*see* light' or to '*hear* sound'. These latter words suggest sensation rather than intellectual discernment. If so then Farmer's argument, when applied in the case of holiness, would make it a quality in very much the same sense as 'whiteness' or 'greyness' is a quality, and I have already argued against this supposition. But if Farmer were to vote for the other alternative, then it seems to me that he could have put his point over in a much less misleading way by saying plainly that being aware of God is like intellectual discernment. I have myself conceded that intellectual discernment is, in some ways, like sensation, and if being aware of God is like intellectual discernment then it fol-

22

lows that being aware of God too is in some ways like sensation, so that we need not entirely disagree with what Farmer says if he were prepared to accept this interpretation.

I would reformulate the argument of Farmer and Baillie as follows. Knowing, or being aware of God, is like what I have called intellectual discernment, and in so far as the latter is similar in some respects to sensation so knowing, or being aware of, God is like sensation too. But when the argument is put in this way it seems to me that to compare knowing God with sensation is much less to the point than to compare it with intellectual discernment. It is along these lines that I see any future for the argument, and if understood in this way it may tell us something about holiness.

The suggestion we are now left with is that holiness may be the object of something like intellectual discernment, of 'seeing' in the second of the senses of the word which I distinguished above. It is worth noting that a person with good eyesight may look and yet fail to 'see' in this sense of the word. One may look at a chessboard and see all there is on it, but fail to comprehend the significance of the pieces and their positions on the board. Intellectual discernment involves grasping relations and patterns which are sometimes relatively simple and sometimes very complicated. Relations and patterns can even be 'seen' independently of looking at a thing with our eyes; sometimes looking helps, sometimes it is a hindrance, and sometimes the intellectual discernment comes by looking at something other than what we are trying to understand.

Yet, intellectual discernment is not entirely and absolutely independent of sensation. The chess player must either see or feel his board and the various pieces which are on it, and the most complex scientific theories have a firm empirical grounding. We can work back from the most complicated patterns and interrelations which have been intellectually discerned to a point at which something must be perceived with one of the senses. Some of the senses can supplement each other to a remarkable degree, such as in the case of a blind man whose visual sensations are supplemented by tactual and aural sensations, but if we had no sensation whatever, then it is difficult to imagine what intellectual discernment we could have either.

It will be helpful to take up an example at this point. Consider the meaning of the word 'useful'. An example of an object that deserves to be called useful would be a lawn-mower which is in good working order. Now, the lawn-mower's usefulness cannot be seen, in the first sense of the word 'see'; we do not detect its usefulness as we detect its colour, or its sound when working, by sensation. It is in the intellectual sense of the word 'see' that we may be said to 'see' the usefulness of a lawn-mower. We could see (sensation) everything in the machine without 'seeing' (intellectual discernment) its usefulness; to 'see' its usefulness is, in a sense, to 'see' more than the eye as such takes in. Yet, sensation is relevant to this intellectual discernment of the usefulness of the machine, for we could not say that it was useful unless we did have certain sensations. The machine must be seen, felt by touch or perhaps heard at work, and we must know through sensation what grass is like, what the difference is between a smooth and a rough lawn, and a whole host of other things besides. 'Seeing' that a lawn-mower is useful involves our having such experiences, but having such experiences does not constitute 'seeing' (intellectual discernment) that the machine is useful. To 'see' that the machine is useful is to grasp a whole complex of facts, relations and interrelations between facts.

If holiness is something that is intellectually discerned, rather than seen with the eye as a colour is seen, then we should expect it also to be similar in some respects to 'usefulness' for instance. This is indeed so. For holiness too, while not being itself an observable phenomenon, is nevertheless related to certain observable phenomena. Just as usefulness is related to a certain range of observable phenomena, but is itself more than what the eye takes in, so is holiness related to certain observable phenomena, yet is not itself one of them but something more which can perhaps only be 'seen' in the second sense distinguished above.

That holiness does relate to certain observable phenomena can be shown by referring for instance to the *Book of Common Prayer* of the Church of England. In the rubrics relating to the rite of Holy Baptism for example it is specified that the font is to be filled with 'pure water', which suggests that if the water was impure that would somehow or other impair, or distract from, the holiness of the rite. The baptismal rite is not called holy merely because the water that is used for baptism is pure; the purity of the water does not itself constitute the holiness of the sacrament, but it is generally speaking an essential feature which is necessary if the rite is to be holy. Again, the elements in Holy Communion are to be covered with a fair white linen cloth, and the suggestion once more seems to be that the holiness of the sacrament would be impaired if the cloth was not linen, not white or fair. The priest is to minister the bread with 'decency' and the remainder of the consecrated elements are to be 'reverently' placed upon the communion table; indecency or irreverence would thus detract from the holiness of the sacrament. Yet the sacrament is not holy merely in virtue of the whiteness of the cloth, the decency and reverence with which the elements are ministered; in other words, to say that the sacrament is holy is to say more than that the cloth used to cover the elements is white, or that the elements are to be treated with decency and reverence.

There are of course many words like this which, while being related to observable phenomena, refer to something more than what the eye takes in. 'Usefulness' is only one of a host of words which could be compared with 'holiness' in the same way, so this does not take us very far towards understanding what the distinctive meaning of holiness is. Since there is such a great variety of different words that behave in this way, we must try to hit upon those which provide the best clue to the meaning of holiness, and those that are most closely associated with holy situations. Then it is necessary to explore the comparison in each case and to see how far holiness is thus explained, and whether or not something is still left over.

The words that I have chosen for the development of our discussion are 'fearfulness', 'powerfulness', 'wholeness', 'separatedness' and 'goodness'. There are good reasons for picking upon these particular ones as I shall show in each case by scriptural and theological references. None of these words stand for qualities which are appreciated through sensation, like whiteness or greyness. Rather, they are understood by 'seeing' more than just what the eye takes in.

I venture to make one further point here in anticipation of

what I shall have to say later on. It would hardly be possible to give a fair account of 'usefulness' without referring to a purpose which the useful instrument serves to achieve, and though animals have limited purposes it is only by reference to a *person* that we can account for a purpose which involves a thing like a lawn-mower, not to mention more complex machines. Thus we are not likely properly to understand what is meant by 'usefulness' without knowing something about persons, and how complex a question that is can be seen from recent contributions on the subject.[6]

These contributions might however suggest that our awareness of a person involves a discernment which is over and above pure sensation, though, as in the other instances just mentioned, it depends also upon sensation. Furthermore we shall significantly notice that it is when personal reference is drawn into the picture that the discussion of 'fearfulness', 'powerfulness', 'separatedness' and 'goodness' take us furthest towards understanding the meaning of holiness. Indeed, this personal reference will eventually prove to be the master-key to the whole problem.

[6] Such as Professor Ryle's *The Concept of Mind*, Professor J. Wisdom's *Other Minds*, and contributions by Professor J. R. Jones and Mr. T. R. Miles in *Proceedings of the Aristotelian Society Supplementary* Vol. XXX and Professor I. T. Ramsey in the *Hibbert Journal Vol. LIV* or *Philosophical Quarterly* Vol. 5.

CHAPTER III

FEAR OF THE HOLY

HELMER RINGGREN, in his short treatise which is translated into English under the title *The Prophetical Conception of Holiness*, claims that 'that which is holy is also dreadful and terrible'.[1] This claim can be easily supported by appeal to Old Testament texts. I shall quote but one or two—'holy and terrible is thy name' (Ps. 111/9), 'Let them praise thy great and terrible name; for it is holy' (Ps. 99/3), and finally 'O God, thou art terrible out of thy holy places' (Ps. 68/55). Another Old Testament scholar, J. Pedersen, says in the second volume of his work which is translated into English under the title *Israel*: 'this sense of fear is caused by the mighty power of holiness. It surpasses what is *known* to ordinary human beings, hence they cannot control its laws, and do not know whether it will serve to strengthen or to destroy them.'[2]

Two things should be noted here. In the first place, holiness has produced some kind of fear in religious people. It is not easy to say what kind of fear this is, but whatever the experience is like, 'fear' seems to be the word for it, which suggests that in trying to understand what is the nature of people's reaction to holiness we might begin by considering fear-situations. In the second place, we should note at the outset, however, that fear of the holy is not exactly like ordinary fear. There is something distinctive about the religious believer's fear of the holy which suggests that holiness is not quite like ordinary sources of fear. We have just seen that Pedersen describes the source as 'the mighty power of holiness'; it is by no means an ordinary power but a power that *'surpasses* what is known to *ordinary* human beings'.[3] I do not want to consider holiness as a power just yet, but intend in the present chapter to bring out as much illumina-

---

[1] *The Prophetical Conception of Holiness* p. 10 (Uppsala, 1948).
[2] *Israel* III and IV p. 267. (Oxford, 1926).
[3] My italics.

27

tion upon the holy as is possible by concentrating attention upon this element of fear.

It may be just as well to say a word or two about ordinary fear in general to begin with, and then to consider concrete instances. Broadly speaking, one may say that fear can involve either or both of two things, namely (a) an emotional upset and/or (b) a disposition to take safeguarding action. Fear as an emotion is often associated with imminent and obvious danger —a wild animal, or something of the sort, threatening one's life. The situation usually comes to a climax for better or worse, and the emotional strain is tantalizing if the climax is delayed. It is otherwise in the case of dispositional fear. This is a dormant fear; it is a readiness to take precaution and a disposition to have an emotional upset if a fearful situation should arise. I have never met a wild tiger but if I was dumped defenceless in a place known to me to be inhabited by wild tigers I should certainly feel uneasy. Thus it makes sense to say that I am afraid of wild tigers even though I am safe enough and quite unconcerned about them at the present moment; my fear is a dispositional one. A discussion of both the emotional and the dispositional aspect of fear should take us part of the way towards understanding what is meant by the holiness which is the cause of the fear.

FEAR AS AN EMOTION

Let us consider a situation with which we are all reasonably familiar and which might seem to be very similar to the situation referred to in the words which I quoted from Pedersen's book. The example I wish to take is that of a thunderstorm. A thunderstorm gives the impression of there being a mighty power at work, a power over which there seems to be no control, and we can never be sure that the lightning will not strike us with fatal effects. It is by no means obvious that everyone dreads a thunderstorm but some people certainly do, children sometimes do but not invariably, some animals do, and others do not.

It is a well-known psychological fact that action is the best means of allaying fear, and we may assume that the converse of this is also true, that is, that the less one can do to safeguard oneself against imminent danger, the more pronounced will the emotional upset tend to become. In a thunderstorm there is not much opportunity for taking safeguarding action, therefore when fear does grip us it is usually the emotional aspect that is uppermost. As I have just said, not everyone is gripped by fear in an ordinary thunderstorm, but we can easily imagine the elements being intensified to such an extent that terror gripped all but a very few. Moreover, even in an ordinary thunderstorm the bravest of men will feel a shudder if the lightning strikes exceptionally close to him, possibly killing the man next to him. At the least, it is hardly likely that there are more than a very few people who cannot imagine at all what it feels like to be afraid in a thunderstorm.

If anyone was afraid in such a situation then it would be quite understandable, for an uncontrollable, mighty, and partly unknown power would be threatening one's life. It is a situation of very real danger, and we should hardly think of arguing that the terror stricken person's fear was unreasonable, unfounded, or uncalled-for. One should also note the temporary character of such a situation. Thunderstorms do not usually last very long. And if they did, then the longer one survived through them, the more would the emotional aspect of the fear wear off. It is as though nature had given us a safety-valve device which ensured that such a torturing dread kills itself after any length of time despite the continuance of the threatening phenomena.

Let us now ask how similar or dissimilar this fear is to the religious believer's fear of the holy. When the lexicographers tells us that נוֹרָא must be translated 'terrible' or 'aweful' in such cases as Psalm 68/55, 99/3, and 111/9,[4] where the holy is also mentioned, then it might be supposed that there was an emotional element of fear in the Hebrew's encounter with the holy. That is the reasonable conclusion to draw from the choice of the translations 'terrible' and 'aweful'. Now, granted that this emotional aspect of fear does come into the Hebrew's experience in connection with the holy, and granted also that by telling the thunderstorm story along the lines I suggested a

[4] See *Hebrew and English Lexicon* (Ed. Brown, Driver and Briggs).

situation is given which explains one use of the word 'fear', the question arises: but is that word used in *precisely* the same way in connection with a thunderstorm and with holiness? Is it *exactly* the same kind of feature which justifies us in using the word 'fear' in both situations?

If the answer to this question were in the affirmative it might seem tempting to take up a position similar to that which Professor A. J. Ayer took in his book *Language, Truth and Logic*. There he argued that if someone says that the occurrence of thunder is sufficient for him to establish that 'Jehovah is angry' then 'in his usage of words, the sentence "Jehovah is angry" is equivalent to "It is thundering"'.[5] Similarly one might be tempted to say that 'I am afraid because of holiness' simply means 'I am afraid because it is thundering' or something of the sort. Such a view however cannot go without serious challenge, for holiness is not related to a specific set of criteria in the same way as thunder is. This is not to say that holiness is not related to any evidential criteria at all. On the contrary we must admit that it often has been associated with such phenomena as that produced in a thunderstorm for example. Holiness is certainly very closely related with deity in the Old Testament as we shall see later, and God's voice is represented as thunder (see II Sam. 22/14, Ps. 29/31, Job 37/5). There has always been a tendency to associate holiness, and especially fear of the holy, with out-of-the-ordinary phenomena such as thunder or earthquakes. Even as late as the eighteenth century an earthquake was 'for the majority of people an event "instinct with deity", terrible because of the holiness of God'[6] as T. D. Kendrick shows in his fascinating account of the Lisbon earthquake. Indeed, it might be reasonable to conclude from what *some* people have said, and the way that they behaved, that holiness was for them simply another word for these exceptional phenomena. That is, for *some* of the witnesses of the Lisbon earthquake for instance holiness might well be wholly unpacked in terms of the observable phenomena of that earthquake.

There is good reason for believing however that many be-

---

[5] *Language, Truth and Logic* p. 116. (Gollanz, 1946).
[6] *The Lisbon Earthquake* p. 25. (Methuen, 1956).

lievers have meant more than this by 'holiness', and that their fear of the holy should not be identified with their fear of a thunderstorm or of an earthquake. It may be that it was in a thunderstorm that the Hebrew was most afraid of the holy, but still he was not afraid merely and only because of the lightning and thunder. After all, the Hebrew also connected God's presence with very different sets of phenomena. We remember how Elijah in the cave recognized the voice of God not in the wind, the earthquake or the fire, but in the 'still small voice' or as the Revised Version suggests 'a sound of gentle stillness'.[7] Job describes how he feared and trembled when a spirit passed before him and he heard the spirit speak in silence (R.V. margin: 'I heard a still voice').[8] Job feared and trembled, and Elijah hid his face in his mantle, because of something more than any mere observable feature of their surroundings. We all know how awe-inspiring silence can be at times, especially sudden silence after a great storm for instance, but it is not fair to dismiss the experiences of Elijah and Job as being of this kind for they tell us that the silence *spoke* and *sounded*. Their claim is expressed in very paradoxical terms and we often speak paradoxically when we are trying to express something which is both striking and very difficult to express. One cannot hope to express plainly in a few words what Job and Elijah meant here, but I am satisfied just now to emphasize the fact that holiness was not for them the sort of thing that could easily be unpacked in observational terms. It was beyond the phenomena in some sense or other, though also often manifested in them. The holy, whatever it was, was something to be feared, yet not just as a thunderstorm or an earthquake is feared. One could possibly fear an earthquake or a storm without having feared the holy, and one could fear the holy where there was no storm or earthquake, though the two situations could of course also coincide, and have in fact done so. This latter point should not however be allowed to obscure the fact that it is one thing to fear a thunderstorm, but something more to fear that which is holy.

This same point is brought home to us when we consider how the Hebrew associated holiness with fire, cloud and smoke.

[7] *I Kings* 19/11-12.   [8] *Job* 4/16.

The appearance of Yahweh on Mount Sinai was associated with the appearance of fire and clouds of smoke. Again, in the account of the prophet's vision in Isaiah Ch. 6 we are told that the house of God was filled with smoke (v. 4). A cloud also filled the house of the Lord when Solomon's temple was consecrated (I Kings 8/10). Pedersen explains all this by referring to the practice of burning incense. Of the cloud which appeared over the *hak-tappareth* in Lev. 16/2, Pedersen says: 'the cloud is the cloud of incense which the high-priest caused to ascend'.[9] Pedersen also adds, 'here we have the reality underlying the descriptions of how Yahweh always spoke enveloped in a cloud in Mount Sinai'.

If this is so then the fear of holiness which gripped Isaiah, for instance, in the story of his vision in Ch. 6, is not quite like the fear which might be instilled in us by observing the cloud of smoke from a volcanic eruption. The latter would be due to the fact that whatever gave rise to the cloud was beyond our control, and full of threatening possibilities. But the cloud of smoke rising from incense was not beyond the priest's control, and there is no reason to believe that he thought this in itself to be portentous of untold dangers in the same way as a volcanic eruption is. Therefore, the fear of holiness, which is admittedly associated sometimes with clouds of smoke, is not quite the same as the fear engendered by the presence of a volcanic eruption or a threatening storm.

Even if the origin of the practice of burning incense could be traced back to experiences of fear in the presence of dark threatening clouds associated with storms or volcanic eruptions, we should not expect the same fear to be engendered by the artificially created incense cloud. If fear is associated with the incense cloud, as seems to be the case with Isaiah, then this could hardly be the same kind of fear as the ordinary fear of the ordinary threats I have just mentioned. The inevitable conclusion seems to be that this fear which Isaiah experienced in the circumstance described in Is. Ch. 6 was an extraordinary kind of fear altogether. Should it ever be proved that incense burning can be traced back to situations where threatening clouds produced fear, we can argue that possibly even those

[9] *Israel* III and IV p. 247.

first experiences were something more than just being afraid of the immediate effects of a storm or a volcanic eruption. This would be the case in which ordinary fear coincided with fear of the holy, though the latter would still be something over and above the former.

What I have tried to show so far is that fear of the holy does not derive from a specific set of phenomena in the same way as the fear of a thunderstorm, for instance, is caused by thunder and lightning, and that the fear of holiness is to that extent extraordinary. The threats and dangers which give rise to the ordinary type of fear that I have considered are easily located and objectively verifiable, but in the case of holiness it is impossible to locate an extra particular threat or danger which can be verified in the same way. Ordinary reactions of fear are often more or less reflex, and certain threats and dangers constitute the necessary and sufficient conditions for producing them, but we can find no such necessary and sufficient conditions which give rise to the fear of the holy. This is not to say that fear of the holy has *nothing at all* to do with any verifiable conditions whatever, but only that there are no obviously threatening aspects of such conditions that can easily be specified.

A caustic retort is possible here. Someone with a flair for clarity might hold that I have not established anything like an extraordinary fear-situation by this denial of the presence of ordinary objectively verifiable threat and danger. Surely, we meet cases in ordinary everyday life where a person is gripped with fear although there is no special observable danger. Take the case of a person suffering from claustrophobia for instance. The confined space within which the person who has this phobia is afraid constitutes no more of a threat to him than it does to any other person, yet this particular person cannot help feeling afraid in such a situation. There is however, as often as not, an explanation for this person's fear; the psychologist may trace his condition to a childhood experience of being locked in a room for a long period without company, without anyone to give that love and attention for which the child naturally craves. Whatever the psychological explanation may be, if the psychologist can cure the condition, as is the case very often, then the whole situation is cleared and there is nothing extraordinary about it.

Some thinkers might want to argue that religious fear of the holy may be something of this sort. Freud has maintained that religion can be explained away in terms of a projection theory. First of all it is emphasized how a child depends on his earthly father for provision, protection and so forth. Then, as he grows up he still finds that there are uncontrollable elements in the world which make it very difficult for him to fend for himself with absolute security. He therefore still needs a providing and protecting father. The earthly father is now unable to give the son any more than the son can give himself. So what happens is that the son projects his idea of a father who is capable of doing far more than any earthly father could do, a father who is to an adult what the earthly father is to the child, and supposes that there is some actual being corresponding to this idea. A similar explanation might be offered for the religious person's fear of the holy. John Wisdom seems somewhat partial to this Freudian explanation in his article entitled 'Gods'.[10] With reference to feelings of awe and confidence before the gods he writes: 'we have only to remind ourselves of these feelings and the stories of the gods and goddesses and heroes in which these feelings find expression, to be reminded of how we felt as children to our parents and the big people of our childhood'.[11]

It seems to me that these two cases, that of a phobia and that of religious fear, are widely divergent. Instances of the former case are comparatively few, while religious fear is far more general. Cases of claustrophobia often yield to psychological treatment, but the most subtle psychological manoeuvres far more often than not fail to convert a religious believer to infidelity. Again, claustrophobia can be traced back to a fairly definite characteristic childhood pattern. It is not so with religious believers. They are drawn from all ranks; sometimes the believer as a child knew no providing or protecting father at all, sometimes the parents are religious, sometimes not, sometimes cruel and negligent, sometimes kind and protecting. It would be a very formidable task indeed to find any definite

---

[10] *Logic and Language* (First Series) Ch. X ed. A. G. N. Flew.
[11] *Logic and Language* (First Series) p. 203.

specific pattern of circumstances which can be shown to have psychologically conditioned every one who betrays any signs of religious fear, and consequently equally difficult to 'cure' anyone of this fear. I conclude that claustrophobia is altogether a far more obviously pathological phenomenon than the religious person's fear of the holy.

Few would wish to deny that a pathological element is present to some degree in many cases of religious fear, and psychology should be capable of teaching us much on this point. Psychological treatment might well bring about a change in the nature of this religious fear, and possibly remove it altogether in some cases—at least in its cruder forms. But to go on from this to maintain that religious fear of the holy is simply a pathological phenomenon, and nothing more, is to take a very big and unjustifiable step. For this contention to appear plausible we should require a satisfactory and fairly generally accepted theory which accounts for religious fear at least as clearly as some of the recognized psychological theories account for such conditions as claustrophobia. Where have we such a theory? Admittedly, the religious person's fear of the holy may at some points remind us of our childish fear of our parents and various other adult authorities, but this does not explain anything. It is very misleading indeed to jump from this fact of reminiscent likeness to the conclusion that 'the whole thing' (the religious attitude) is 'patently infantile'[12] as Freud does. The fact that as a child I feared my parents does not in itself prove that it is unreasonable for me as an adult to experience fear in what might be called holy situations. Neither does the fact that these situations are very puzzling, and seem to contain no directly verifiable objective threats or dangers, justify anyone in jumping to the conclusion that the religious fear is due to the projection of an ideal authority derived from our childhood guardians.

Furthermore, if this Freudian account is to appear plausible then there should be some recognizable technique of curing religious, so-called pathological, cases. Can psychoanalysis claim fairly general achievements in this respect? Success in a few instances does not prove the case, since it will be readily

[12] *Logic and Language* (First Series) p. 203-4.

admitted from the start by religious people that pathological elements are mixed with, and even mistaken for, religious elements in some cases. The psychoanalyst has a long way to go before he can establish the Freudian projection theory as plausible, and it does not seem to me that he has gone anything like far enough to show that the religious person's fear of the holy is as curable and explicable as pathological phobias.

If fear of the holy is neither ordinary fear—that is, the fear displayed when there is obvious danger—nor pathological fear, then what kind of fear is it? One religious thinker who has made a serious attempt to answer this question is Rudolf Otto. He discusses the question in the aforementioned book—*The Idea of the Holy*. 'This "fear",' Otto maintains, 'is more than fear proper.'[13] With reference to Old Testament expressions for this feeling he writes, 'here we have a terror fraught with an inward shuddering such as not even the most menacing and overpowering created thing can instil'.[14] Otto tries to bring out the unique character of this extraordinary fear by using, and discussing the use of, such words as 'awe', 'daemonic dread', 'uncanny', 'eerie', 'weird', the Greek σεβαστός and the German 'erschauern'. He compares and contrasts various states of fear, and tries to show which are nearest to, and which are furthest from, the unique fear of the holy.

Not all the critics of Otto have recognized his emphasis on the unique and extraordinary character of the fear which relates to holiness. Consider for a moment Dean Inge's comment in his essay which is published in *Science and Religion*. Dean Inge says that 'Otto is right in emphasizing the feeling of awe, dread and fascination as an essential part of religion', but adds, 'it is generally mixed with superstitious elements, and should never be the dominant feeling in the approach of the Christian to his Father in heaven. "He that feareth is not made perfect in love".'[15] These last few words show that Dean Inge has not understood Otto to be referring to the fear of the holy as an unique and exceptional kind of fear at all, for the 'fear' mentioned in the verse which Dean Inge quotes is surely anything

[13] *The Idea of the Holy* p. 13.
[14] ibid. p. 14.
[15] *Science, Religion and Reality*. p. 377-8. (Sheldon Press, 1926).

but the fear of the holy. There may be certain kinds of fear which are cast out when we have perfect love, but the fear of the holy can hardly be one of those. This latter is a fear to be commended and encouraged; Job is commended as a man that 'feared God' (Job 1/1) and when God is worshipped in the 'beauty of holiness' we ought to 'tremble before him' (Ps. 96/9). *This* is the fear of the holy, and we are never to grow out of *this* fear, though the presence of God does cast out *other* fears, such as the fear of earthly enemies (see Ps. 27/1).

Dean Inge has not found in Otto's descriptions anything more than a reference to an intensified form of those ordinary fears which should wither away in the presence of God. But Otto himself was intending to draw our attention to the extraordinary fear which will always be with us when we are in the presence of the holy. Although Otto did refer to ordinary kinds of fear in his attempt to make us understand what the fear of the holy is like, he was always careful to emphasize that this latter kind of fear is not exactly the same as the others. This emotional response is, according to Otto '*wholly distinct* from that of being afraid, though it so far resembles it that the analogy of fear may be used to throw light upon its nature'.[16] A little later he refers to it as 'a feeling of *peculiar* dread, *not to be mistaken* for any ordinary dread'.[17] Again, still engaged in the quest for the special meaning of 'fear' in the holy context he writes: 'of modern languages English has the words "awe", "aweful", which in their *deeper* and *most special* sense *approximate* closely to our meaning'. Otto could hardly make it plainer that the fear of the holy is not just ordinary fear and nothing more. But does he give us any positive indication of what this extra-ordinary fear is like, and of what its source is like?

There are one or two suggestive points in Otto's account which, it seems to me, could be made the starting point of a more positive discussion. Consider first of all Otto's discussion of the Greek word σεβαστός. This, says Otto, is a title 'that could not fittingly be given to any creature, not even to the emperor'.[17] This way of putting it seems to suggest that, though the emperor is not worthy to be called σεβαστός yet he is

[16] *The Idea of the Holy* p. 13.   [17] ibid. p. 14.

nearer to it than those that belong to the category of 'any creature'. This in its turn seems to imply that σεβαστός was at least a personal title. Otto could still preserve his emphasis on the difference between the person who was worthy of this title and any others, such as the emperor, and something more would have to be said about how even the word 'person' was used in such a context. But such a step would take us a little further than the ground which Otto actually covers.

The second point at which Otto could have made a similar development in his theme is in his discussion of ὀργή the 'wrath of God'. This he tells us, is something which belongs to the objective side of the numen, or the holy, but again Otto's own attitude is disappointingly negative. He says that ὀργή is 'quite wrongly spoken of as "natural" wrath', and that it is 'an entirely non- or super-natural i.e. numinous, quality'.[18] Otto might have given more prominence to the personal reference which seems to be so essentially implied in this word 'wrath'. It would indeed have to be shown that the 'person' in this case was a quite exceptional person, but this would seem to be a more promising line of discussion than Otto's, which only emphasizes again and again that the holy is *sui generis*.

I would suggest that we should think of the situation in which the Hebrew or Christian worshipper finds himself when he fears the holy as being in some ways akin to that in which someone is aware of the presence of a person who has great power and authority over him. Sometimes the fear in question is not so much like the fear of a person who exercises great power of authority over us, but more akin to the kind of awe which is sometimes engendered by great love. One may still stand in awe of a parent when he has ceased to be in a position of power and authority over us; a profound, awesome respect for him can result from our knowledge of his deep, sincere love and concern for us, and the fear of the holy is in some ways akin to such awe. It is certainly not so much a case of being afraid of something which is causally connected in an obvious way with death or injury. It is a case rather of being confronted with a person such that the last thing one wants to do is to cross his will. Present-day Christians claim that they some-

[18] *The Idea of the Holy* p. 19.

times find themselves in a similar situation, and experience a similar fear, yet the phenomena associated with this type of situation have varied greatly and the emotions aroused are not precisely the same every time. Much seems to depend on religious people's views about the person whom they take to manifest himself in these situations, and those views have varied with place and time. Furthermore, religious fear of the holy is not always unmixed with other fears, especially in the case of primitives.

Clearly, the 'person' whom the holy situation bespeaks is no ordinary person for he is not to be recognized by his facial features like other people nor is his presence signified by private belongings such as a hat or umbrella, but by thunder, clouds of incense, gentle stillness and so forth. Certainly more needs to be said about the 'extraordinary person' involved in the holy situation if my suggestion is to be fruitful; so far I have only introduced the suggestion in connection with the emotional aspect of the fear of the holy. Would it be relevant in a discussion of this fear considered in its dispositional aspect?

DISPOSITIONAL FEAR

It was the emotional aspect of the fear of the holy that was foremost in the above discussion, but as I have hinted already, there is another aspect of the religious believer's fear of the holy which must be brought out. To go back to Hebrew religion, it would be wrong to imagine that when the Hebrews talked of fearing the holy they were merely referring to exceptional emotional upsets such as that suggested by our thunderstorm example. Thunderstorms come and go, and the fear connected with them is a correspondingly temporary affair. The Hebrew's fear of the holy was something more than a temporary affair like that: the holy was not entirely an episodic affair, but something more constant and everpresent.

Take the case of the holy ark for instance. This holy object was not to be touched by a profane, unsanctified person on pain of suffering death. As long as the ark was in the possession of the tribe it was a constant source of danger and therefore constantly to be feared. This constant fear was not an everpresent emotional state, but rather a disposition to behave in certain ways with respect to the holy ark. If we are to understand what holiness means in this context then we must see how the disposition in question is related to the observable situation which can be described in terms of the ark and its environment, and one way of finding this out is by comparing this situation with another and seeing whether the disposition is explained in the same way in both cases. The ordinary everyday case which I wish to bring up for comparison is that of an electrician's fear of touching an electrically charged wire.

It was apparently thought by the Hebrews that if a profane person touched the ark then death would follow automatically. There springs to mind the comparable fatal effect of touching an electric wire carrying a heavy electric current. Moreover, the danger would be a constant one where one would fear to touch the wire, yet having no positive emotional upset at all. Part of an electrician's job, for example, might be to manoeuvre his hand dexterously amongst a complex set of live wires and terminals. He is extremely cautious because he dreads having an electric shock which might be fatal. Yet the wires will do him no harm until, or unless, he touches them. They do not go for him or seek to encompass his hands like tentacles. Thus there is no need or desire to remove the source of danger as there would be where there is a direct menacing threat to life such as when one is attacked by a wild animal for instance. Far from it being desirable to remove the source of danger in our example, it is highly desirable to keep it for the sake of its valuable uses. So long as electricians are careful, the power with which they deal is extremely serviceable.

Similar points can be made regarding the place of the holy in the life of the Hebrews. Wheeler Robinson says that 'sacred objects can be touched only under the strictest precautions; they are as dangerous to the uninitiated as the switchboard of an electrical power-house might be to a child'.[19] Yet the holy was not necessarily a source of danger and nothing more; it wasn't simply a threat which it would be desirable to remove from their midst. On the contrary, holiness could be a source of blessing, success and life. The ark, which could be the source

[19] *The Religious Ideas of the Old Testament* p. 131 (Duckworth, 1921).

of such destruction, was also a source of blessing while it rested in the house of Obed-edom (II Sam. 6/11). Pedersen says, in his account of the Hebrew sacrifice and its effects, that 'if all holiness vanished, life would perish because the blessing draws its nourishment from holiness'.[20] It was therefore a far more indispensable source of blessing to the Hebrews than electricity is for modern civilization but, as Helmer Ringgren says, 'this presupposes that that which is holy should be handled in the right way and that he who approaches it should be well prepared to do so'.[21] Precautions such as changing, washing clothes, taking off shoes, must be observed lest the holy should prove fatally hostile. So long as certain rules were kept everything would be all right. Some might wish to claim, mistakenly as I hope to show, that these precautions were comparable in all respects to the electrician's precautions.

Let us follow the possibilities of the comparison further. The electrician is not in a state of conscious fear or experiencing an emotional upset while going about his work, yet he would protest actively and violently if someone tried to push his unprotected hand on to a heavily charged terminal. He is afraid, and constantly afraid, in this sense. That is, what he has is not so much a constant fearful emotion as a constant disposition to behave in a certain way in relation to the electrically charged objects, and to have certain emotions of fear when something goes wrong, when for instance there is a short-circuit and a normally dead wire might now be alive. Exceptional precautions are then necessary.

The Hebrew's relation to the holy was very similar. He was not consciously afraid all the time, and at most times his fear of the holy amounted to a disposition to have fearful emotions and to behave in certain ways in relation to holy things and places. As often as not, at any rate while he behaved in the commendable manner specified in the Hebrew law, the Hebrew's emotional state in relation to the holy was one of calm confidence. We may quote Pedersen again in this connection. He says, 'the more man was able to enter into spiritual relationship with holy things, the more did his dread of their holiness

[20] *Israel* III and IV p. 299.
[21] *The Prophetical Conception of Holiness* p. 10.

disappear'.[22] Thus the Hebrew's relation to the holy had two correlative aspects: (a) fear when it threatened to be a danger, and (b) confidence while the holy gave blessings. Whether things went the one way or the other depended in some way upon the behaviour of the Hebrew himself. In all this the Hebrew's reaction to the holy appears at first sight to be rather like the electricians attitude in dealing with electricity.

There is one further point that can be drawn out by reference to our model. The apprentice electrician soon acquires a calm confidence and goes about his work without the conscious fear of touching live wires which might be evident at the beginning of his career. Sometimes however, the youngster can become over-confident, completely oblivious of the danger involved in his work, and then it is necessary to conjure up the old emotion of fear once again. His superior tells him about the disastrous effects of an acquaintance's carelessness in a similar situation. One hopes that the novice will be more afraid next time and, consequently, not so careless. There is reason to believe that the Hebrews often became similarly over-familiar with the holy. This was probably what gave point to the prophet's reminder that God was dreadful in his holiness (Cf. Is. 29/23). It may have been partly the purpose of the narrator who wrote such stories as those of Uzzah's death, and the destruction of the men of Beth-shemesh, to regenerate the fear of holiness which the people were inclined to forget. Naturally the whole cultic system also tended to guard against fearless over-confidence in the people's approach to the holy, and to reinforce the appropriate fear and dread.

It might seem from all this that we are well on the way towards understanding what the Hebrew's fear of the holy was like, and what the holy itself was like, but attention must now be drawn to some important differences between the two cases we are considering. The electrician knows that if he touches a live wire he will get a severe electric shock which might be fatal. He is quite sure of this, and knows that it will happen without fail whenever someone touches the live wire. But, on closer inspection we see that it is not quite the same in the case of things that are feared for their holiness.

[22] *Israel* III and IV p. 270.

We have one classic example of a person dying immediately he touched the holy ark just as though it were charged with a power very similar to an electric charge. I am referring to the case of Uzzah whose story is given in II Sam. 6/6 ff. But let us look closer at the whole situation. The first thing to note is that the holy ark could cause death by means other than contact. The men of Beth-shemesh died because they *looked* into the ark. (I Sam. 6/19). We do not die merely by looking at an electrically charged object. It is only by contact, or in some cases proximity, that an electric charge can kill. At this point it becomes extremely plausible to offer natural accounts of the death of Uzzah and the men of Beth-shemesh. We have plenty of examples of people suffering instantaneous death by straining themselves when they have a weak heart. Such an explanation would fit the evidence in the story of Uzzah's misfortune very well. As to the men of Beth-shemesh, they may well have been killed in battle with the Israelites.

Moreover, we know that in some cases whoever touched a holy thing was to be put to death by stoning or shooting with an arrow (Ex. 19/12,13). If death by contact had come automatically upon touching the holy object as it does upon touching a wire which carries a heavy electric current, then there would be no need to shoot or stone the offenders. They would already have suffered their penalty automatically. So it does not seem at all likely that there was any real danger of automatic death immediately a holy object was touched. It should also be noted that in the case of both Uzzah and the men of Beth-shemesh, the claim of the narrator is that *God* smote them. Presumably God smote them because they touched, or looked upon, the holy ark, but this need not imply that God smote them by means of the touch or look. This suggests that though holiness is mediated through things, yet it did not reside as a quality in things. The Hebrews would not have commented in the case under discussion 'look what the ark has done', as one might say 'look what the high-tension circuit has done' where death followed touching a charged piece of electrical wiring.

Thus we are quite sure that there is a real danger corresponding to the electrician's fear of touching live wires, but we are not anything like so sure of the nature of the danger which corresponds to the Hebrew worshipper's fear in the presence of the holy. There is no systematic chain of evidence in connection with holiness which is comparable to the systematic chain of evidence available where there is danger of an electric shock. There are reliable theories which enable us to predict the effects of touching a live wire, and every time a live wire has been touched the effects have confirmed the truth of the relevant theories. There is no comparable theory of holiness to consider. When we approach such stories as those of Uzzah and the ark in a scientific frame of mind then the only explanation that sounds plausible is something like heart-attack or thrombosis.

Someone might now suggest in an easy-going fashion that the Hebrew simply mistook naturally-caused death for the supposed extraordinary effect of the holy ark, and that now, since far better explanations are available, we should treat the Hebrew fear of the holy as groundless. But this view does not take account of the fact that the Hebrew tribe in some cases *inflicted* a death penalty for touching the holy. This latter fact suggests that some more far-reaching consequences were feared than anything that might befall the individual offender himself. The Hebrew's fear of the holy was like the electrician's fear in that it involved a disposition to behave in a certain way with respect to certain situations, and to be even emotionally upset if anything went wrong, but the objective character of the threat or danger is not tractable in scientific language. There is something very puzzling here; there is something exceptional about this holy fear-situation.

There is also the other side of the picture. Like the electrician, the Hebrew worshipper could be calm and confident in his relation with the holy as long as certain codes of behaviour were respected. But here also there is a significant difference between the two cases. The electrician's precautionary behaviour, and resultant confidence, are based upon a scientific understanding of the nature of electric currents and charges. Since there is no comparable scientific understanding of the holy, the question arises of how the Hebrew decided what would be a safe code of behaviour, and also how he acquired his calm and confidence. When Pedersen talks of entering into a 'spiritual relationship with holy things'[23] what are we to understand by the words 'enter into spiritual relationship'? It is this word 'spiritual' that makes it all so difficult. There is nothing in the electrician's situation that will help us to understand that. Once again we are puzzled; there is something strange here.

Finally, the electrician knows quite well how and in what ways electrical power benefits us, but it is not anything like so clear how, and in what ways holiness benefited the tribe. We are indeed told that 'the Lord blessed Obed-edom, and all his household' (II Sam. 6/11) while the holy ark rested there, but these words take us far away from the sort of definite, tractable benefits that we derive from electricity. The kinds of benefits that we derive from electricity can be enumerated, we can explain how electricity provides them, and can say what benefits are *not* produced by electricity. The Hebrew could admittedly refer to material benefits which he would call 'blessings', but to call such benefits 'blessings' and to attribute them to 'the Lord' is not to give the same sort of scientific account for them as we can give of the benefits which we derive from electricity. What could be more unscientific than this word 'blessed'? And who is 'the Lord'? If we approach this aspect of the holy situation in the scientific frame of mind we are simply baffled; our categories will not apply.

Thus, if we want a good example that will help us to understand the dispositional fear of the holy we require one where, firstly, it is believed that if certain things were not done then danger would arise from a certain source, and if other things were done benefits would flow from this source. Secondly, it must be one wherein the threats and benefits are not scientifically calculable and explicable. It seems to me that the most fitting example is that in which the source of threat or benefits is believed to be a person. We can well imagine ourselves having a dispositional fear with respect to a person of great authority and power upon whom we were dependent. We should avoid doing certain things which we thought contrary to his will lest he should take revenge upon us by cutting off from us some of the necessities of life for which we depended

[23] See *Israel* III and IV p. 270.

45

upon him. Yet we should not, in such a case, think that the deprivation of necessities followed automatically in a scientifically explicable way. Neither would we think that the behaviour which we imagine the person of authority to require of us brought benefits in an automatic way. We should certainly entertain beliefs about the person in question, and hold certain views as to the sort of behaviour that would be likely to secure his favour or evoke his anger, but such beliefs would not be scientific hypotheses.

It seems to me that the dispositional fear of the holy which the Hebrews manifested can be understood better in the light of this example. This personal model also sheds some light upon the fact that dispositional fear was also closely associated with emotional fear, and especially reverence, in the experience of the worshipper. Yet, obviously the personal example that I have suggested would have to be qualified if it was to fit the case exactly. The personal situation that is required to account for the Hebrew's dispositional fear of the holy must be an extraordinary one altogether. This person would have to be an *absolute* authority and *all*-powerful, but here again the question arises: what do we *mean* by the word 'person' in such exceptional circumstances?

Mention must now be made of another example which no doubt suggests itself to some people as promising to throw light upon the Hebrew's dispositional fear of the holy. The example I now have in mind is that of superstitious belief and practice. These beliefs and practices constitute very bad science, indeed they do not deserve to be called scientific at all though they sometimes seem to pose as such. They are often expressed in the form of hypotheticals, like many scientific statements, but they are not subjected to the stringent tests whereby scientific hypotheticals win respect. Superstitious hypotheticals are usually so general that anything could be picked upon as answering to the consequent. Take, for example, the supposition that if I walk under a ladder bad luck will follow. Obviously, this term 'bad luck' could be given a very wide interpretation so as to include almost any slight mishap, yet superstitions are like scientific hypotheses in that they betray a desire on the part of those who believe in them to control their environment. Conditions which cannot be directly controlled are connected with events which we can determine; for instance, bad fortune which we cannot *directly* avoid is connected with going under ladders which we can avoid.

It might be held that the Hebrews were very bad scientists trying to make sense of their environment and to bring it under their control, but whose efforts, appear to us today as groundless superstitious beliefs. Here we have a tribe of people who were well acquainted with adversities coming their way through the force of circumstances over which they had no direct control—a most distressing experience. The adversity could be something as terrible as defeat in battle by a cruel oppressor, and for the individual there was the last enemy of death itself—sometimes coming unexpectedly and untimely. These were things that would naturally distress the Hebrews as they would, and do, distress us today. Next, we know that it is a fact that these people did connect such fatal events as these with the breaking of rules relating to the holy. The account of Uzzah's death is a case in point. If he had not touched the ark he would not have died, presumably. Again kings were anointed and soldiers were consecrated to their task, for it was believed that if these things had not been done then there was no guarantee of victory in the battlefields.

These rules specified points at which the tribe and the individual could control things. For example Uzzah could not have avoided dying once he touched the ark, but he could have avoided touching the ark. That was a point at which he could have controlled his own fate. Similarly a tribe which disrespected the holy could not hope to win a battle but it could have been more observant of the demands of the holy, thus its fate in battle was, in an indirect way, in its own hands. All this, it might be held, is just superstition to be treated on a par with the case of believing that walking under ladders is connected with misfortune. If so, it would seem that holiness was pure fiction.

It cannot be denied that there is some force in this argument, but I would like to suggest that there is more even to superstition than we sometimes realize. It is possible to interpret superstition as being a crude and misinformed attempt at scientific explanation, but this need not be the whole story, so I would like to offer a different interpretation. My point can best be brought out with the help of a specific example.

Consider the case of a man who has missed a train-connection with consequent great inconvenience throughout his trip, and who attributes this piece of misfortune to the fact that he had walked under a ladder a few days previously. When this man comes home after his unhappy journey, he tells his family the whole story including the bit about the ladder. His sophisticated son rejects this superstitious nonsense and, having unbounded faith in his own newly discovered powers of reasoning, he takes his father to task regarding the latter's credulity. The son tries to make it clear to his father that the cause of his missing the connection could be traced without reference to walking under ladders at all. He suggests that there may have been a fog preventing the connecting train arriving at Oxford on time. It is hardly likely that the father, with all his credulity, would want to deny the possibility of there being some such natural cause of the train's delay, but he might well ask: 'but why should there have been a fog just at that particular time on that particular night?' and he might add, 'I tell you, it is my going under the ladder that's behind it all.' The son counters doggedly with a reference to further natural causes of the fog, such as atmospheric conditions and so on. 'Yes,' the father replies, 'but why should it happen that the whole system of atmospheric conditions should be so arranged that a fog forms at precisely the right time and place to upset the timing of this particular train that would have taken me to my connection?' He is more certain than ever that he shouldn't have walked under the ladder. What is evident by now is that the father is interested in something more than the natural or scientific explanation of the sequence of events. When all such explanations have been given he still wants to ask: why? And since it is not a scientific answer that the question now requires what other sort of answer could we have?

Sometimes, when we ask 'why?' what we require is not a natural explanation of why certain events followed the course they did but an explanation from the person responsible for the state of affairs in question. What I now want to suggest is that the father's attitude in my example can be understood as tacitly assuming that there is a 'person' of some kind who is responsible for the universe and who could give his personal reason for making it what it is. Such an interpretation will also account for the man's attributing his misfortune to the fact that he walked under the ladder. This would be understandable if the man was under the impression that going under the ladder was objectionable to the mysterious 'person' who controlled his fate. We could then see the man's way of reasoning even if we disagreed with some of his premises. Many religious people would indeed disagree with this man's premises. While agreeing that there is a 'person' of some kind who somehow 'controls' the world, and who is interested in our behaviour, they would hold that he is not the crude primitive spirit whose reactions depended on such trivial matters as our walking under ladders. He is a higher being who is interested in our behaviour in a different way.

Superstitions may contain the germ of a more sophisticated faith. If we reject the idea that the 'person' who is somehow responsible for the universe is affected by our walking or not walking under ladders, we can still believe that there is a 'person' of some kind who is somehow responsible for the universe, and that some forms of human behaviour are not in conformity with such a person's principles. We can reject the superstitious person's crude assumptions while still retaining something of his attitude. This is the attitude that we find in Hebrew religion too, and is perhaps retainable even though we reject some of the crude Hebrew assumptions that were once associated with it.

This, I would suggest, is the attitude which lies behind the dispositional fear of the holy. It is an attitude which assumes that there is some kind of 'person' somehow responsible for our life and environment, a 'person' with whose will our life should accord if we are to flourish and not perish. Certain places, times, objects and people are considered to be related to this 'person' in such a way that any disrespect for them offends the all-powerful 'person' himself. They are therefore held in awe and reverence, not just on account of a quality or property inherent in themselves, but because they are peculiarly related to an extraordinary person. The thunder was the *voice of the Lord*; the curious box that should be handled with such great respect was the *ark of the Lord*, and the holy of holies was the place of *His presence*.

It seems that holiness belongs to a situation where, firstly, certain natural features are regarded as having a special significance. Secondly, such features are talked about in a way which would only be apt if they were somehow associated with an extraordinary personal presence. Finally, it is characteristic of such a situation that it engenders an emotion or disposition best described as fearful. Since we are all familiar with clouds and thunder, as we are also with fear, it is tempting to go straight on to consider the extraordinary and unfamiliar personal aspect of the situation in which these familiar phenomena become impregnated with holiness. Clouds, thunder and fear are not however the only features associated with it, so other approaches are possible to the question: what is holiness? It is only when these other approaches have been tried, and shown to involve reference to an exceptional kind of 'person', that we should go on to consider what more can be said of such a person.

CHAPTER IV

THE POWER OF HOLINESS

ANY plausible discussion of holiness will have to give a
prominent place in its vocabulary to the word 'power'. I have
already referred to Pedersen's description of the source of
religious fear as being 'the mighty power of holiness',[1] a description which immediately suggests that holiness is a power of
some kind. Wheeler Robinson tells us that 'the earlier idea of
"holiness" . . . is that of inaccessibility, perilous and unknown
power',[2] and however much the concept of holiness was subsequently modified power is still associated with holiness in the
Christian tradition too. The Holy Spirit, according to Cyril of
Jerusalem, is 'a mighty power, divine and mysterious'.[3] The
view that holiness is a power of some kind is confirmed by the
fact that the Hebrew God, who was sometimes referred to as
'The Holy One', (Is. 40/25) was also called 'the power', ἡ
δύναμις, (Mt. 26/64 and Mk. 14/62). As T. W. Manson says
' "The power" means simply God'[4] in these contexts. Since 'the
power' and 'the Holy One' have been used for the same being—
God—we may infer that the two terms mean very much the
same thing. It is interesting to note that the Hebrew 'El, which
in its plural form 'Elohim came to stand as the usual name for
the Hebrew God, may have been used for someone whose chief
characteristic was great strength. We cannot be certain of this
but Oesterley and Robinson go so far as to say that 'in the
course of time it is likely enough that 'El came to connote one
who was strong'.[5]

From all this we might conclude that the words 'holy' and
'holiness' are logically comparable to the words 'power', and

[1] See p. 27.
[2] *The Religious Ideas of the Old Testament* p. 69 (My italics).
[3] Quoted from *Introduction to the Early History of Christian Doctrine*.
By J. Bethune-Baker p. 207. (Methuen, 1933).
[4] *The Teaching of Jesus* p. 266. (Cambridge, 1935). See also *The Names of
Jesus* by Vincent Taylor for the same view. p. 150. (Macmillan, 1953).
[5] *Hebrew Religion* p. 52. (S.P.C.K., 1949).

'powerfulness'. They have been to some extent and with certain qualifications exchangeable in religious discourse, but the qualifications are important. It will not do to substitute the word 'power' for 'holy' in all contexts and to carry on as though the two words meant precisely the same thing, for when reference is made to holiness as a power then the word 'power' is almost invariably qualified. This power is called 'mighty', 'unknown', 'mysterious', 'divine'. In the above example (Mt. 26/64 and Mk. 14/62) where God is simply called 'the power' there is indeed no qualifier present, but the use of the word as a personal title preceded by the definite article is enough to put the term on a logical pedestal of its own. Such an use presupposes that there is no other power like this. This must be an extra-ordinary power, different from all the ordinary instances of power that we have. It is not sufficient therefore to grasp the general meaning of the word 'power' in ordinary discourse if we are to understand its significance when it is associated with holiness.

I must therefore consider the various ways in which the word 'power' has been qualified in religious discourse. Then I shall attempt to show how holy power belongs to a situation where physical power *is* manifested, but where something extra is *also* involved. This theme I shall then further develop with special reference to the Hebrew conceptions of life and wisdom.

QUALIFIERS

It might be thought highly desirable that what I have called the ordinary use of the word 'power' should be crisply and clearly delineated, before any qualifiers are brought into the picture. But if this were possible it would benefit a strict positivist far more than the philosopher of religion. It will not behove the latter to ignore such emancipating contributions to recent philosophy as Dr Waismann's emphasis on 'open texture',[6] for instance. Therefore, let us not try to pin down too definitely an ordinary use of the word 'power'. Even ordinary power situations vary enormously, and this makes it very difficult to specify any definite common characteristic in virtue of which

[6] See article 'Verifiability' in *Logic and Language*. (First Series) Ch. VII.

the word 'power' becomes appropriate to the various situations.

Yet, although we cannot give a clear definition of ordinary power or prescribe a precise use for the word, we can say enough to satisfy the child or man in the street who wants to be able to incorporate the word in his practical vocabulary. Consider one or two fairly common, well-known, ordinary power-situations. There is the case of mechanical power, such as when we speak of the power of an engine; there is also the power of an electrical charge and even the power of light. In these cases we can refer to definite phenomena which provide evidence for the existence or non-existence of those powers—the car moves, the battery produces electrical effects, the light shines with a certain intensity. This kind of power can also be measured in terms of horse-power, voltage, or candle-power respectively. This does not complete the story by any means. Much more can be said and probably ought to be said in certain contexts but it is not to my purpose to continue the story any further than this; the important thing is that we now know how to go on with it, what branch of science to study if we want to know more about it. There is much to learn about power in this sense, but most of us already know enough for practical purposes, and probably have a sufficiently secure footing on this particular linguistic ledge to make further advances. Here are instances of generally *recognized* power-situations with a generally *recognized* method of scrutinizing them further.

Consider another case, namely, that of political power. This can also be given an unpacking in terms of strategical position, population, mineral wealth and so forth, or again, in terms of majority votes. It turns out to be a long story if anyone should ask us more about it, and a philosopher of religion would hardly be the most inexhaustible narrator. Still, as in the other instance, we know enough to recognize a situation as one of political power, and we know whom to interrogate if a fuller account is desired. This power-situation is different from, and possibly more complex than, the first we mentioned but not sufficiently so for us to call it extraordinary.

These examples of ordinary power-situations could obviously be multiplied. There is the power of a voice, or of an organ, in the sphere of music; the power of a blow or a shot in the sphere of sport; while in sailing we may talk of the power of a breeze or of a current. All these are ordinary uses where it is possible to explain very easily what is meant to an ordinary man in the street and to tell him where to go for further information if he is interested.

Holiness as a power is not quite like those I have just mentioned, and it is not comparable to them in being empirically verifiable in the same way. That is why it is necessary to bring in qualifiers such as 'mighty', 'mysterious' and so forth, where the context itself does not make it sufficiently clear that the word 'power', when associated with holiness, is being used in an extraordinary way. It will be worth considering the function of these qualifiers in more detail.

Taking the word 'mighty' first, we have to agree that the word could be used of physical powers such as that of a jet-engine, or a hydrogen bomb, but when the word begins to be used of such powers then we are ceasing to think of them as scientifically measurable and calculable in their effects. That is why the word would sound just that little bit more appropriate in connection with the hydrogen-bomb than with the jet-engine. To describe a power as being mighty is to suggest that it is getting beyond measure, that it is incalculable, that its effects are a matter of open possibility. Thus to call the power of holiness 'mighty' begins to shut it off from comparison with many instances of physical power. Yet this does not take us far enough, for holiness is not straightforwardly comparable to any physical power whatever—not even the power of the greatest hydrogen-bomb. The virtue of the word 'mighty' is that it can be used to suggest this as well, for we can always shoot beyond any particular example of a mighty power by talking of a power that is mightier still. There is a limit to such a power as that of the hydrogen-bomb; we know that even if the whole earth was devastated by its effects there will still be other planets and certainly other galaxies that will not be affected by it. But why shouldn't someone maintain that when he called the power of holiness 'mighty' he meant that it extended beyond *all* limits? There is no reason why the word 'mighty' should not be pressed this far, and it seems to me that it is only when power is called 'mighty' in this extreme sense that it begins to serve as a guide to the nature of holiness. For it should be remembered that the 'Holy One' of Israel was also called the '*Most High*' and '*almighty*' (Numbers 24/16).

The word 'unknown' can qualify in a similar way. This word can of course be used in a quite straightforward way to say of power that it is unmeasured, or it could be used to say of a power that it is from the practical point of view immeasurable. This need not mean that there is any theoretical difficulty about the measurement. The power of the electrical charge of a cloud in a thunderstorm could theoretically be measured, though it is in practice well nigh unmeasurable. We could, however, use the word 'unknown' to suggest that the power in question was such that we had no idea how to set about measuring it or calculating its effects. The power of holiness would be such; it is unmeasurable even in theory.

This point is perhaps better emphasized in the next qualifier —'mysterious'. When the detective pronounces that a certain crime is a mystery, he is not referring to the practical difficulties of applying a certain theory, but to the problem of inventing or establishing a theory to account for the puzzling facts. The scientist does not call a situation mysterious merely because he is up against a practical difficulty in applying a certain model explanation. A situation becomes a mystery for the scientist when he finds that his model does not work, does not apply, and he feels constrained to invent a new one. The word 'mystery' indicates a point at which our present state of knowledge and understanding comes to a dead end. In such fields as science and crime-detection an advance is often made beyond these points eventually; new explanatory models or theories are evolved and detectives hit upon solutions in the case of the most ingeniously executed crimes. No mystery then remains; it was only a temporary mystery.

Some mysteries are greater than others. Scientists and detectives more often than not deal with local mysteries, but we are on a very different plane when we speak of the whole universe for instance as being mysterious, as it was from the point of view of so eminent a mathematician and astronomer as the late Sir James Jeans. We might think of a mystery which is beyond all mysteries, such that to solve it would be to solve everything, and it seems to me that the mystery of the power of holiness is like that. It is a mystery that remains when every other partial mystery has been solved. If the power of the holy is mysterious in this sense of the word, then it must be a very extraordinary power indeed.

The last of the qualifiers that I have mentioned is the word 'divine'. This word immediately suggests that the power of the holy is not an ordinary physical power of any kind. We should hardly think of characterizing a physical power as divine unless perhaps we wanted to say that all power is divine in the last resort, but the point of using the word even then would be to indicate that physical power is something more in the last analysis than we usually take it to be. I shall indeed suggest shortly that holy power can in a sense be manifest in a physical power. Certainly to call anything divine is to indicate that it is not of this world as ordinary things and powers are of this world. It is to relate the thing in question, in our present case power, to a being that we call God. This accords with the contention that I have previously made, namely that 'the power', where it can stand in the place of the 'Holy One', is God. Thus we begin to see how questions about the holy become convertible into questions about God—a point that will have to be taken up in further detail later.

PHYSICAL POWER AND 'MORE'

Now that the discussion has been taken to this stage one might be left wondering whether or not 'power' in this exceptional sense has anything at all to do with power in its ordinary sense. I have emphasized the difference between ordinary power and the holy power so much that it might easily be forgotten that this word 'power' is after all one and the same word in the very different contexts. It would therefore seem that despite all that has been said so far there should be some kind of connection between the holy-situation and an ordinary power-situation, otherwise why use the word 'power' at all in the first case?[7] So I want to make a claim here which should not be misunderstood as being concerned with establishing anything like a straightforward philosophical continuum wherein a description of an ordinary power-situation leads easily on to a description of a holy power-situation. My claim is that we cannot talk of a holy power-situation without reference to ordinary power-situations any more than we can, for instance, talk of a person in complete abstraction from his body and observable behaviour. We must not think that there are two situations—the holy and the ordinary—any more than a person is one being and his body another, neither should we think of the holy as being a spatio-temporally unearthed location within the ordinary situation any more than we should think of a human mind as being a ghost situated within the human machine. Yet it must be remembered that we shall miss the mark if we talk of holy power as though it were an ordinary instance of power and nothing else.

Consider for a moment the power of the Holy Spirit of which we hear so much from the author of the Book of Acts and Saint Paul. The English word 'spirit' here translates the Greek word *pneuma* and C. H. Dodd tells us that 'the Hebrew word which corresponds to *pneuma* has the meaning "strong breath", or "blast",[8] and he further adds that 'the idea of power is inseparable from it'.[9] Thus we are taken back to a situation whose main obvious feature was a blast of wind, and this would be as good an example of ordinary power as anyone could wish. The situation seems quite 'down-to-earth', yet it is evident that

---

[7] Cf. what Hare says in *Language and Morals* pp. 118-9 and 145-50. (Oxford, 1952) about the possible changes in the meaning of the word 'good'. Of course, he makes it clear how this word can have such different uses without becoming a different word by pointing out that it is only the descriptive meaning of the word which changes, whereas the commendatory element remains constant throughout. It is not so easy however to distinguish the elements which change from the others which remain constant when the word 'power' is put to the different uses under consideration.

The point I wish to make here is not unlike that made by A. N. Prior in his book *Logic and the Basis of Ethics* where he criticizes the tendency of what he calls 'therapeutic positivism' to fix upon one usage of the word 'good' instead of furthering philosophical enquiry with an open mind into the possible range of usages, and into the possibility of there being a common characteristic in all cases where the word is used. (See *Logic and the Basis of Ethics* p. 10-12. (Oxford, 1949).

[8] *Romans* (Dodd) p. 117. (Hodder & Stoughton, 1949).

[9] *ibid* p. 117.

when the Hebrew associated holiness with such a situation he 'saw' more in it than just what the eye took in, more than its observable phenomena. Then we remember how 'thunder was, by common consent, the voice of God', [10] and how Job asked: 'but the thunder of his power who can understand?' (Job 26/14). The power exhibited in a thunderstorm was as closely related with holy power in the Hebrew mind as was the power of a blast of wind. In Psalm 104/7 we read: 'at the voice of thy thunder they hasted away', and in verse 4 the psalmist says: 'who maketh winds his messengers' or as the Revised Version also suggests—'who maketh his angels winds'. We need not think that a voice was heard in the middle of the thunder nor that the thunder was articulate, and it would not do to say that 'voice' here simply means 'thunder'. The writer is not referring exclusively to ordinary thunder or to an ordinary voice either, but to a situation to which he can only refer in the way he does. Similarly it is not just ordinary messengers or ordinary wind that the psalmist is thinking of when he talks of God as the one 'who maketh the winds his messengers'. The mistake of trying to identify this situation as a natural one wherein 'voice' simply means 'thunder', and 'messengers' simply means 'winds', should be obvious if we remind ourselves of the story of Elijah in the cave where the holy presence is not in the wind nor the earthquake nor fire but comes in a 'still small voice' or as the Revised Version suggests: 'a sound of gentle stillness' (I Kings 19/11-13).

Other examples can be given where the Hebrew associates the power of the Holy One with concrete empirical situations. The escape of the Jews from Egypt through the Red Sea was a situation that could be described in terms of empirical phenomena, but the Hebrew 'saw' more in it than that. He 'saw' that situation as exhibiting the divine, mighty power of holiness; it was God who had saved the tribe 'for his name's sake, that he might make his mighty power to be known' (Ps. 106/8). This power was not a particular power that could be exhaustively described in terms of the observable phenomena of the escape through the Red Sea, but the *al*-mighty mysterious, power of

[10] *Readings in the Fourth Gospel* by William Temple, p. 198. (Macmillan, 1950).

God. As Reinhold Niebuhr says, the Hebrew God was thought of as 'being the source of all power, and not some particular power in history'.[11] Yet, as I have been trying to show, this power was very often closely associated with physical power as well. My point could be summarized in Niebuhr's own words: 'power is the product of Spirit. It never exists without an alloy of physical force but it is always more than physical compulsion'.[12]

If I am asked how one can 'see' more in a thunderstorm, for instance, than what is perceived with the eyes and ears, then it is not easy to answer but the following analogous case taken from a very different sphere may help. Consider Edward Lockspeiser's description of *Namouna*, by Edouard Ialo, in *The Listener*.[13] In trying to describe it he refers to what he calls 'its *unrelenting*, persistent rhythms and its *wild* fanfares on trumpets'.[13] He also comments that *Namouna* is 'a very *powerful* work, much *bolder* in colour than . . .' and 'undeniably *human*, *vibrant* and alive'.[13] Would another music critic have described his impressions in precisely the same way? We should hardly expect so. A very complicated account, and possibly an useful one for some purposes, could be given of the performance in terms of vibrating reeds, resonance chambers, wave frequencies and so forth, but this long story would not satisfy the music critic, not because it cannot be completed or taken far enough, but because it misses the point from the start. Similarly we could tell a complicated story dealing with electric charges, heat, violent air movement, sound waves and so forth, and try to exhaust the thunder situation in this way. But again we might well be missing something, not because the story is incomplete and cannot be taken far enough, but because the whole language is inappropriate.

Yet it would be a mistake to think that the ordinary power situation can be completely ignored and forgotten when we refer to the power of holiness. H. H. Farmer comes dangerously near to doing this at a certain point in his book *Revelation and Religion*. After referring to a certain section of Hadfield's *The*

[11] *The Nature and Destiny of Man* Vol. II p. 23. (Nisbet, 1943).
[12] *ibid.* p. 21.
[13] *The Listener* Vol. LIV No. 1399 p. 1101.

Psychology of Power, where he deals with human power, Farmer says: 'the facts are well enough known, and, though they certainly reveal mysterious, unfathomable powers in man, in themselves they no more point to a religious interpretation of man, nor require a religious attitude for their understanding and control, than do the mysterious powers which reside at the heart of the atom'.[14] On the view I have been trying to put forward, it must be quite otherwise. It is easier to agree with Paul Tillich who maintains that 'even in the structure of the atom there is something primordial, a Gestalt, an intrinsic power'.[15] Not always does Tillich succeed in making his discussion of such terms as 'intrinsic power' particularly lucid, but some light is thrown on the minimum content of his claim here when he says in the same context that 'the rational objective view of nature is . . . never fully applicable'.[16] The implication is that there is more to the story of the atom than the physicists are capable of telling us, and even this story, when taken far enough, might awaken an awareness of holy power. One would expect that this would be even more true of the powers of a human personality—powers which we shall certainly have to consider in more detail later on.

Yet there is a sense in which one could agree with Farmer. If he wishes specially to emphasize that the divine power is not an extention of human power or a parallel to it, such that a psychologist could account for it in the same terms as he accounts for human power, then his point is valuable. One can also agree with Farmer's condemnation of deliberate attempts to induce speaking with tongues and certain Yoga practices which are psychological phenomena and certainly not religious.[17] The power of holiness is not a thing to be measured in terms of such phenomena as these, though we have to be careful here too. C. H. Dodd tells us that the power of the Holy Ghost in the early church 'found expression in apparently supernatural phenomena like "speaking with tongues" and "mighty works",'[18] but he does not give us any room to think that the

---

[14] *Revelation and Religion* p. 181. (Nisbet, 1954).
[15] *The Protestant Era* p. 112. (Nisbet, 1955).
[16] ibid. p. 112.
[17] See *Revelation and Religion* p. 182.
[18] *Romans* (Dodd) p. 118. (Hodder & Stoughton, 1949).

power of the Holy Ghost should be conceived as being analysable in terms of the 'speaking with tongues' and 'mighty works'. 'Paul had experience of these abnormal manifestations of "spirit", but he found that beneath them there were "gifts of the spirit" more real, more important, and more enduring—namely, intellectual and moral endowments for the service of God in His church, and, above all, the divinely given power to live after the pattern of Christ'.[19] Possibly, psychological and scientific accounts could be given of the 'speaking with tongues' and 'mighty works', but such accounts would not cover the 'divinely given power' which Paul found beneath the overt wonders. These strange happenings were, for him, occasions which brought with them an awareness of a 'divinely given power'.

In view of this we must criticize Harnack for complaining that the common life of the Church 'no longer possesses "the Spirit and power" '[20] when his ground seems to be simply the fact that the church does not perform miracles and speak with tongues as it once did. Harnack either mistook the wonder-works for the power of the Kingdom, or else he must have thought that the wonder-work is an *essential* feature which must be present whenever the power of holiness is at work. Professor S. H. Hooke makes clear the difference between miracle-power and the divine power in his book entitled *The Kingdom of God in the Experience of Jesus*. For example, he shows how the leper (Mt. 8/1-4) 'believed that power was available, but he thought of it as a wonder-worker's power, . . .' and how Jesus 'was distressed to find the forgiving and healing power of the Kingdom so meanly thought of'.[21] It is the failure to recognize the wonder-work as exhibiting also a divine power that is distressing. Thus we see how it could be possible for a person to be within a 'mighty works' situation and yet to miss the Spirit and the power—that is, the divine power of holiness. This fact should convince us that there is no *essential* connection between 'mighty works', or 'speaking with tongues', and

[19] *Romans* (Dodd) p. 118.
[20] Quoted from *The Expansion of Christianity* in *The Faith that Rebels* by D. S. Cairns p. 28. (S.C.M. Press, 1933).
[21] *The Kingdom of God in the Experience of Jesus* p. 52. (Duckworth, 1949).

divine power. The latter can be present in the absence of the former, and other situations can today be the occasions of our becoming aware of divine power.

Compare a miracle with a thunder situation. We can imagine a child wondering at a thunder situation, but seeing nothing in it when later in life he becomes acquainted with the scientific explanation of the event. But suppose someone becomes aware of divine power in the thunderstorm, then this awareness can remain even when the physical manifestations had all been explained. Similarly a miracle could be an occasion of someone's becoming aware of the divine power, and this awareness could persist even when the miracle is explained scientifically. The first person would tend to refer to the divine power in terms of thunder, the second in terms of a miracle, but it would be wrong to think that either of them was thinking simply of thunder or simply of a miracle as such. The very earliest disciples quite probably thought that mighty works were *essential* manifestations of divine power, but there is no reason to deny that they had at the same time a real awareness of divine power. There is no reason why we should not have a similar awareness in other situations today, and it seems that part of the purpose of church ritual, worship and preaching should be to evoke this awareness. Therefore when Harnack points out that 'the common life of the Church has now its priests, its altar, its sacraments, its holy book and rule of faith', he should *not* have added, 'but it no longer possesses "the Spirit and power" '.[22]

LIFE AND HOLY POWERS

Holiness as a power has been especially associated with life in its various forms. For the Hebrews, holiness was the source of all life and was quite indispensable for its continuance. Following Pedersen's interpretation of Hebrew religion, we read : 'in the old days there was always a possibility of holiness where there was soul life : in the life of the spring, the stone, the tree, in the life of animals and human beings. All forms of life

[22] Quoted from *The Expansion of Christianity* by Cairns in *The Faith that Rebels* p. 28.

draw their growth from holiness, because their vital force emanated from it.'[23] Was holiness then thought of as being an occult cause of life? Were the Hebrews trying to formulate a crude scientific explanation of life when they thought of it in terms of this 'vital force'? If that was all they were doing then one might indeed justifiably point out that modern science has swept all such old-fashioned notions clean off the board. The present-day scientist claims that everything can, in principle at any rate, be fully explained with no remainder. Charles Sherrington writes, 'Natural science has studied life to the extent of explaining away life as any radically separate category of phenomena. The categories of living and lifeless as regards science disappear; there is no radical scientific difference between living and dead.'[24] If there is no more to such situations than what science could tell us, then the supposition that there exists a power of holiness is as outmoded as the phlogiston theory.

The Hebrew was not, however, trying to give anything like an explanation of life that would satisfy the queries of a scientific mind, and it is not as a crude scientific hypothesis that his view of holy power should be understood. It must always be remembered that the Hebrew's thinking was 'not theoretical, but of a pronouncedly practical character'.[25] The Hebrew was not inclined to make logical deductions within a situation but to lump together the complex impression which he received, and the associations of his ideas were not therefore necessarily logical but reflections of the impact which the various aspects of the situation made upon him. The question of whether there was anything that we might call a logical, or scientific orderliness about those associations did not bother him. 'The Israelite does not argue by means of conclusions and logical progress. His argumentation consists in showing that one statement associates itself with another, as belonging to its totality.'[26] Thus, when the Hebrew holds that a life situation is also a holy power one, he is *not* arguing that because the situation is A it must be also B; rather, he is presenting the situation

[23] *Israel* III and IV p. 286.
[24] *Man on his Nature* p. 239. (Penguin, 1955).
[25] *Israel* I and II p. 126.
[26] *ibid.* p. 115.

as it strikes him, that is as AB. He is reacting to the life situation as it strikes him in its totality and, it would seem, it strikes him as being the observable situation it is for everyone, but also something more.

Consider the Hebrew worshipper's attitude to the 'blessing' (berākhā). This Hebrew word for 'blessing' was used to refer to a power which saturated the soul—'this vital power, without which no living being can exist, is called by the Israelites berākhā, blessing.'[27] The Hebrew had another word for the ability or power to live, namely 'sālāh' which also appeared as 'hisleāh' and this word referred to living in the sense of succeeding or prospering. According to Pedersen, 'this word thus means the same as blessing. It designates the efficiency as an inner power to work in accordance with its nature, and at the same time success, prosperity and the carrying out of that for which one is disposed'.[28]

There is a double reference involved here, one being very much an observational matter whereas the other is not. Success, prosperity and the carrying out of that for which one is disposed, are very down-to-earth matters which one could measure in terms of observables. Prosperity could be measured in terms of the number of cattle owned, or the size of the flock or the extent and quality of the vineyard. But the 'inner power', 'the vital power', which enabled one to achieve all this was however more than could be measured in this way. One could indeed, if one chose, think of this power as being correlated precisely with one's material prosperity, and then it would be measurable like the power of a car engine. Moreover, to say that such and such power operated in so and so's farm would be precisely the same as to say that the farm carried this or that number of sheep, cattle and so forth. The 'inner power', 'vital power', 'blessing', or the power of holiness, was much more than this however, though it is not easy to say what more.

We are given a clue however by Pedersen when he says[29] that understanding, or wisdom, was the same as 'blessing'. The implication of this is that one should think of the power in

[27] *Israel* I and II p 182.
[28] *ibid*. p. 196.
[29] *ibid*. p. 199f.

personal terms. Two points should be noted about our use of
the words 'wisdom' and 'understanding'. Firstly, we must admit
that empirical evidence is relevant when we want to decide
whether or not these words are applicable. Secondly, wisdom
and understanding are usually attributed to someone or other.
It is a person that is wise, or if we describe a plan for instance
as being 'wise' then we think of the plan as being the plan of
such and such a *person*. There would be something extremely
odd, self-contradictory perhaps, about talking of a 'wisdom'
that is nobody's 'wisdom', or of an 'understanding' that is
nobody's 'understanding'.

Let us consider a watch as a typical creation of intelligence,
insight and understanding. One interesting point here is that
our view of the watch as being a creation of intelligence is not
derived by inference. On the contrary, the watch is seen from
the start as a piece of intelligent workmanship, and it would be
most difficult to see it differently. A further point to note is
that there is a whole host of statements describing how the
watch came into existence which are *not* entailed by the statement that it is a creation of intelligence. When it is claimed
that the watch is the creation of intelligence, understanding,
insight and so forth, nothing is implied as to precisely how
certain metals were separated out and refined, or how certain
finger muscles and arm muscles moved, or even how certain
brain cells reacted. An account in such terms of the whole complex process involved in the production of a watch would be
very interesting from some points of view. The more detailed
the account became, the more interested the specialist scientists
would become and the more they would have to say as the
account touched upon various specialized fields. But such an
account could be elaborated indefinitely without intelligence
or understanding being mentioned at all. When we do mention
these then a language shift is made; the account moves to a
different plane.

It seems that certain situations struck the Hebrews as being
personal, and exhibiting wisdom and intelligence. We have no
reason to think that the early nomad, wandering with his tribe
through arid deserts and coming round now and again to a
green oasis where life flourished, reasoned and inferred that

there must be an intelligent, powerful person to account for the existence of such a wonderful manifestation of life. On the contrary it seems far more likely that from the first impact the situation was seen and taken as the creation of a personal intelligence.[30] No doubt their notions about such a personal intelligence were often crude, but something of their attitude remains alive in Christian believers to this day. People still find themselves unable to get away from the conviction that behind the incredibly complex patterns of the living universe there must exist a super-human intelligence and wisdom. The Hebrew often thought of this wisdom as being powerfully exhibited in the vital force of life; the disciples of the early Christian church thought of it as being especially manifest in the Spirit which came upon them on the day of Pentecost. This 'wisdom' could, for the Hebrew too, become manifest in the life and history of the individual. To live in accordance with this 'understanding' and 'wisdom' would involve doing something more than just living in the light of our own light and wisdom, and the Hebrew believed that the 'blessing' (which means the same as 'wisdom') 'comprizes the power to live in its *deepest* and most *comprehensive* sense'.[31] Thus 'blessing' is something not entirely unlike human wisdom, but is nevertheless far more. Much more will have to be said later about this divine, personal 'power', or divine 'wisdom', and about its creative relation to the universe.

In the meantime I must take up another point which suggests itself here. When mention is made of a power to live, and more especially a power to live a special kind of life, it is natural to

---

[30] It is worth noting that even Hume, in the *Dialogues concerning Natural Religion* seems to concede that nature strikes us from the first as bespeaking an intelligent person. He puts the following words into the mouth of Cleanthes: 'Consider, anatomize the eye: Survey its structure and contrivance: and tell me, from your own feeling, if the idea of a contriver does not immediately flow in upon you with the force like that of a sensation.' (*Hume's Dialogues*: N. Kemp Smith p. 191). Again in Part XII of the Dialogues Cleanthes is made to say: 'The comparison of the universe to a machine of human contrivance is so obvious and natural . . . that it must immediately strike all unprejudiced apprehensions, and procure universal approbation.' (ibid p. 267). Cf. what Elliot urges Hume to reckon with, namely, with 'the dictates of feeling [i.e. with the immediate impression made upon the mind by the contemplation of Nature] as well as with the conclusions of reason . . .' (*ibid*. p. 111).

[31] *Israel* I and II p. 199. (My italics).

recall other powers which are often connected with special patterns of living. One that suggests itself is will-power, and since we often tend to explain certain aspects of our life in terms of will-power, it might be expected that the power of holiness too is something similar to will-power. I now turn to consider this in the following chapter.

CHAPTER V

WILL-POWER AND LOVE

IT is worth taking note again of Pedersen's contention that holy power is especially a power of living in its 'deepest and most comprehensive sense'. This suggests that we should look beyond that kind of life that is shared by plants and animals and human beings equally and alike. When such phrases as the one quoted above are used it is the morally good life, that life which has the highest value, that is usually in mind. Thus it seems that holy power is not only a power to live, but is especially a power to live a morally good life. This is precisely what is claimed for the holy spirit, which is also referred to by Professor Dodd as 'divine power'.[1] Speaking of the 'genuine action of the Spirit', H. A. A. Kennedy says that it is 'a power for worthy living'.[2] John Calvin described the holy spirit as 'the *Hand* by which God exerts his power because by his divine inspiration he so breathes divine life into us, that we are no longer acted upon by ourselves, but ruled by his motion and agency, so that everything good in us is the fruit of his grace'.[3] I now want to consider how the word 'power' is to be understood in such contexts as these. What do we mean by 'power' when we speak of a 'power for worthy living'? I believe we can go part of the way towards answering this question by considering what is meant by, firstly, 'will-power' and secondly, the 'power of love'.

WILL-POWER

It is well-known that there is a difference between knowing what is good and being able to achieve it. We often know quite well what we ought to do, but do not seem to have the power

[1] *Romans* (Dodd) p. 117-8.
[2] *The Theology of the Epistles* p. 91. (Duckworth, 1948).
[3] *Institutes* Vol. I. p. 465. (T. & T. Clarke, 1949).

to do it. It is in such situations that we confess to having a weak will, whereas the person who is able to do what he knows he ought to do in the face of obstacles is characterized as having a strong will. But what exactly do we mean when we talk in terms of 'will-power', 'strong will', 'weak will'? Take the term 'strong will'. We might think of a man's strong square jaw, or of his perseverance in overcoming a certain particular difficulty, his firm decision in favour of an uninviting project, his general tendency to do his duty even in the face of obstacles and temptations, or his general tendency to persevere with any task once he sets his hand to it. All this would probably lead us to expect similar undaunted perseverance and unflinching decision from the same person in the future, and when we say that a man is strong-willed these anticipations are relevant as well.

Strength of will usually implies all these things, yet it is doubtful if, when we speak of a 'strong will', we simply have these in mind and nothing more. Set jaw, hard decisions, and perseverance constitute very good evidence for a man's being strong willed, but it would be another thing to contend that all we mean when we say a man has a strong will is that his jaw is set, his decisions hard and his perseverance dogged and so on. The sentence 'this man has a strong will' is not simply a shorthand way of saying 'this man's jaw is set and/or he often does such and such or usually does such and such, and therefore I expect him to behave in this way in the future'. The situation is not as simple as that.

There are situations in which we are not simply interested in what a person does or can do, but also in the question: why is one particular person capable of so much more than another? And the statement that a man is strong-willed is not so much an answer to the question: how does this man behave? It looks more like an answer to the question: how is this man able to behave as he does? Why should one person, more often than not, keep his most difficult resolutions whereas another fails every time? It is in giving an answer to such a question that one would talk in terms of will-power.

Some people would maintain that the same answer could be given equally well in biological terms, and that will-power is nothing more than a biological drive. In a paper entitled *The Psychology of Levels of Will* which appeared in the *Proceedings of the Aristotelian Society* of 1947-8, Margaret Masterman (M. M. Braithwaite) attempts to construct a psychology of will which could equate it with the biological 'drive' of development, or growth. She believes that the 'supposition that the will "is" growth, taken psychically, and that growth "is" the will, taken biologically' could bring a 'general clarification in depth-psychological thinking'.[4] 'For,' she adds, 'not only does it provide a clue to a possible scientific justification for the traditional volitional terminology, but also, if the supposition should really turn out to be well-founded, it would at last enable biological drives and psychological instincts to be connected up together by a one-one correspondence, as Freud from the beginning hoped they would be.'[5] The biological concept of growth has an empirical basis in the world of observable phenomena, and Margaret Masterman's suggestion is that the psychologist could appropriate this category and safely equate it with the 'will'.

If Margaret Masterman's case is plausible then the words 'will', 'will-power', 'strong will', 'weak will', would be technical terms with a fairly precise meaning. They would be firmly anchored in the realm of the empirically verifiable. It is not for me to deny the possibility of giving the words such an anchorage with a good use in an explanation which had scientific rigour. Still, to prescribe an use for the words in this way is a very different thing from discovering what the actual usages of the words are. It seems to me that when people explain human action in terms of will-power, they are doing something more than giving a scientific explanation. It is, of course, true that we often do talk of will-power as though it were a sort of force, fund of energy, by which the strong-willed man is able to carry through his difficult projects. It is as though decision and perseverance were made and sustained in virtue of a certain power produced by a little power unit situated somewhere within us, and some people, so it would seem, have a much larger power unit than others. Yet, of course we know quite

---

[4] *Proceedings of the Aristotelian Society* Vol. XLVIII 1947-8 p. 78.
[5] *ibid.* p. 78.

well that there is nothing of the kind situated within any human body. It is only a way of talking, though a way of talking that makes it worth while asking why we do talk like that.

When we speak in terms of will-power we are not usually offering a scientific explanation which is to compete with those already in the field and we are not necessarily denying the validity of any such explanations that may be relevant. The biologist, physiologist and psychologist can indeed tell us much that is useful about human behaviour. What we do intend to affirm however when we attribute strong will-power to a person is that such explanations as the biologist and so forth can offer us are inadequate as final accounts of the whole situation. For instance, let us say a certain person, being very hungry and without food for many hours, makes a very great effort and overcomes great obstacles to secure himself some food. We might say that there was a display of will-power here or, what is rather more likely, we should say that his hunger drove him on to overcome difficulties which would in the ordinary way discourage him. It is indeed more likely than not that the fair explanation of this person's behaviour under these circumstances would be in terms of a combination of hunger-drive and will-power, but it is important to realize that the one explanation is usually meant to cut the other out to some degree. The more we emphasize that it was just hunger that drove the man on, the less ready we are to claim that the person had strong will-power, and conversely, the more we emphasize that the person had will-power the less the significance we attach to hunger as an explanation of the man's perseverance. We emphasize will-power when we feel that such explanations as hunger-drive are inadequate as a total explanation of a person's behaviour. This goes for other cases where the explanation might be in terms of sexual-drive, or of fear. These are the sorts of explanations that would be offered in accounting for animal behaviour, and in these cases we would be very reluctant indeed to make any mention of will-power. Whenever will-power is emphasized then we certainly mean to deny that these alternative explanations are adequate. The situation is felt to be such that something more is involved than just instinct, or organic impulses.

71

If one day we all became quite convinced that all human behaviour can be completely explained in terms of instinct, or biological drives, would we still have a use for the term 'will-power'? I think not, and incidentally this is what the defenders of free-will have always maintained. If explanation in terms of instinct and biological drives were everything then we should feel like saying that man is not what we have always thought him to be; we should then think of him as a depersonalized automaton, and this would have its inevitable consequences in our whole manner of dealing with each other. As it is, we find it very difficult to think of each other as beings whose behaviour can be exhaustively accounted for in scientific terms. Personal contact and interchange is so direct, and the scientific behaviouristic approach so complicated and round-about, that we simply do not think of each other as mechanically conditioned like the electric brain which is so cleverly constructed, but equally cleverly understood. But if we did persist in thinking that man and his behaviour are completely explicable in scientific terms and forgot that there is anything more to it than that, then we would be in danger of losing the capacity for personal rapport and discourse. We are reminded of Charles Darwin's loss of taste for poetry, music and beautiful scenery.[6]

Perhaps the force of the term 'will-power' could be brought out better if we considered it in conjunction with purpose. Purposes can be classed as high or low levelled according to whether they are immediate and closely related to bodily desires or far-sighted and related to the total life of a person or, at a higher level still, with the total life of society. Furthermore, purposes could be classed as high or low according to our value judgements. We generally associate strong will-power with the achievement of a higher purpose in spite of temptations to pursue a low one. For instance, we all know of the temptation to pursue an immediate but transitory pleasure at the expense of labouring at something which will bring a more

[6] It might indeed be argued that our Western civilization is fast moving in the direction of this depersonalized atmosphere—witness such books as Aldous Huxley's *Brave New World* and George Orwell's *1984* and, though I am not entirely partial to the views of such teachers as Martin Buber and his followers, I would hold that such works as *I and Thou* are not without their very urgent message.

lasting happiness in the end. When a person overcomes such a temptation and persists with his difficult task while ignoring his lower desires, we call him strong-willed.

Most of us have to exercise will-power in this sense at some time or other, but we soon get into the habit of living at a certain definite level which varies with different people. Even those who set themselves very high standards in their youth, very often come to a 'plateau' stage in middle life beyond which they show no particular desire to rise. When a person comes to this stage one would be disinclined to say that he exercises much will-power. Hard decisions are over and life has become more a matter of habit. Would we ever say of such a man that he exercised strong will-power? We should probably be most willing to do so if he succeeded in breaking away to some extent from his former pattern of life in order to achieve a still higher purpose, if he sacrificed still more of his immediate desires, or even his higher principles, in favour of a yet deeper insight into a more far-reaching, all-embracing purpose. If a man simply follows a fairly set pattern of life and does just what we expect of him then there is no occasion for talking of will-power. We should not say of the average Britisher who gave up his seat to his elder in the bus that he exercised great will-power. For a clear example of will-power we might refer to Arthur Koestler's action when he cut the bridge between himself and the past by burning all his educational certificates, or to Dr Schweitzer's decision to take a medical course with the intention of going to serve African natives. These are the sorts of behaviour-situations we are usually looking for when we want examples of 'will-power'. They are obviously the situations which are least explicable in scientific terms whether psychological or biological; they are apparently the least predictable kinds of behaviour. This again is perhaps what the defenders of free-will have been arguing for.

Now, is the power of the holy spirit like will-power? Is it the same kind of situation that is appropriate for the mention of both? Certainly, holy power is like will-power in that its meaning cannot be exhausted in terms of instincts or biological drives. Furthermore, what appears to some people as mere will-

73

power has been understood by others as manifesting holy power. Just as thunder, wind, and life have been regarded by the Hebrew as manifesting the power of holiness, so also situations in which will-power was evident have been understood by many people as manifesting the power of holiness too. This is as much as to say that though human will-power is more than just instincts or biological-drives there is a higher power that is even more than human will-power. There are situations which cannot be exhaustively accounted for in terms of *human* will-power.

People who have clearly shown themselves to be weak-willed have been known to change radically and to behave in a way which suggests that they had a tremendous store of will-power. In such cases people have been inclined to say that the power has come to the person from somewhere else, and amongst religious believers it is natural to name God as the source of such a power. A clear example would be the case of the Apostle Peter. His denial of Christ after he had shown that he knew and believed that Christ was his Lord, and had promised to follow him unto death, shows him up as a weak-willed man, but his subsequent testimony in the face of trials shows him up in a very different light. In the New Testament the change is attributed to the descent of the Holy Ghost upon him at the Pentecost.

One could point out that it was otherwise in the case of St Paul, that he was just as strong-willed before his conversion as after, the only difference being that his will came to be exercised in a different direction. Yet, even so, and granted that Paul was a man of strong will-power before, as after, his conversion, he always attributed his power to someone other than himself.[7] Speaking of Paul's experience of abnormal manifestations of the 'spirit' C. H. Dodd says: 'but he found that beneath them there were 'gifts of the Spirit' more real, more important, and more enduring—namely, intellectual and moral endowments for the service of God in his Church, and, above all, the divinely given power to live after the pattern of Christ'.[8] After referring to the life of wisdom and perfection, a life after the pattern of Christ, Paul adds: 'whereunto I labour also, striving

---

[7] See II Cor. 12/10.   [8] *Romans* (Dodd) p. 118.

74

according to his working, which worketh in me mightily (R.V. margin "in power")'.[9]

For such people as St Peter and St Paul the moral situation is often such that a person knows what he ought to do, yet he has not the power and vitality to accomplish it. The holy power-situation is that in which one has the power to achieve the moral aim, but attributes that power to a source outside oneself. There is a vivid reference to this situation in L. S. Thornton's early book *Conduct and the Supernatural*. He discusses the views of such humanist thinkers as H. G. Wells and Bernard Shaw, and he also considers Nietzsche's argument which leads to the idea of the superman, with a view to showing in the end that 'in the search for the foundations of conduct one is driven from the natural to the supernatural'.[10] He holds that the natural order 'contains in itself certain possibilities of moral achievement which it is unable to realize'.[10] Then he goes on to picture the Natural Man, presumably the creation of Wells and Shaw, or Nietzsche's superman, as a plant which is unable to bear the weight of its own growth. The objective moral law is like a high wall up which the plant is to climb, but the tragedy is that the plant has not the requisite strength and vitality to climb that wall. Thornton is certain that 'some superior vitality must enter the plant, in order that it may be able to climb to the heights now required of it'.[11] It is here that the 'supernatural Gospel of Christ' comes into the picture.

All this does not imply that ordinary descriptive accounts of this situation are not relevant, or that religious language is concerned to challenge the truth and value of such accounts at their own level. The situation is not a non-earthly, non-material one. 'For us,' says Thornton 'the spiritual is still in a certain sense within the phenomenal.'[12] He also adds: 'we have to live in a world of sense with our sense-windows opening upon it'.[13] Yet, 'the Power which enables us to move along lines of spiritual activity proceeds wholly from that other-worldly centre where our life is hid with Christ in God, but this Power

---

[9] Col. 1/29 Cf. 1 Cor. 2/5, 11 Cor. 4/7.
[10] *Conduct and the Supernatural* p. 153. (Longmans, 1916).
[11] *Conduct and the Supernatural* p. 154.
[12] *ibid.* p. 176.
[13] *ibid.* p. 176.

has to be exercised in the phenomenal world upon the natural plane'.[14]

Thornton does not wish to deny the scientific student of human behaviour his say given in physiological or even psychological terms, but what he does clearly maintain is that such accounts are not exhaustive and cannot do full justice to the total situation. The man who 'moves along the lines of spiritual activity' is certainly indulging in observable behaviour within an observable world, yet this 'activity' is more than just what can be seen or described, and that is why we need to speak of a supernatural power in connection with it. The term 'spiritual activity' which Thornton uses here throws a further light on the logic of 'supernatural power'. If the situation in which we spoke of 'supernatural power' were capable of being accounted for completely in terms of ordinary observable phenomena then 'supernatural power' could be nothing over and above a biological drive or something of the kind, but the situation is not such at all. The words 'spiritual activity' which Thornton uses indicate clearly that it is an extraordinary situation, and we are led to realize that the 'supernatural power' which is its source is extraordinary. Thus the term 'supernatural power' has an extraordinary logic such that it would be a bad logical mistake to mention this 'power' and then to speak of voltage or horsepower in the same breath.

It is also important to notice how the personal element enters into Thornton's way of speaking of this extraordinary situation. What sort of life is that which 'moves along the lines of spiritual activity'? Thornton says that it proceeds from the centre where our life is 'hid with Christ in God'. Thus to understand this life properly involves knowing something about Christ, the person who lived in Galilee, yet not simply the visible Jesus of nineteen centuries ago but Christ 'in *God*', that is, Christ in so far as he is a divine, supernatural person. He is the clue to the whole situation and to the supernatural power of which Thornton speaks, and this is in keeping with the other indications that we have already had that our enquiry must eventually come to grips with this question of what can be meant by a supernatural, divine, person.

[14] *Conduct and the Supernatural* p. 176.

Nowhere is it more clearly emphasized that worthy living involves a super-human, divine power than in the teaching of St Augustine, who says that 'the human will is so divinely aided towards the doing of righteousness that, besides being created with the free choice of his will, and besides the teaching which instructs him how he ought to live, he receives also the Holy Spirit'.[15] Even sinners and non-believers who become converted are moved towards conversion by the grace of God. He says, having such persons in mind, that 'the wills of men are *prevented*[16] by the grace of God, and that it is God who makes them to will the good which they refused'.[17] Of the saints he says: 'their will is so kindled by the Holy Spirit that they *can*, just because they *will* and they *will* just because *God works in them so to will*'.[18] St Augustine does indeed seem to reserve a place for human will as well when he says of those who receive divine assistance, 'it does not follow that they will not have free choice because sins will have no power to attract them. Nay rather, it will be more truly free, when set free from the delight of sinning . . .',[19] but on the whole the emphasis seems to fall heavier on the compelling power of what he often calls divine assistance. While in this mortal state we are all weak and infirm, and according to St Augustine our only hope is God's irresistible grace. It is not enough that the grace should be there in case we happen to wish to avail ourselves of it; rather, it must force itself upon us and compel us to will that which is good. We are told that 'for them that were weak he (God) reserved his own gift whereby they should most irresistibly will what is good, and most irresistibly refuse to forsake it'.[20] St Augustine does not seem to think that any good can come out of the human free will; it is not free unless it moves us to righteousness—'how can a will be free if it is under the domination of unrighteousness'[21]—but it cannot move us to righteousness without divine assistance which, however, guarantees that we 'most irresistibly will what is good'.[22]

[15] *Documents of the Christian Church* p. 77. (Oxford, 1954).
[16] 'Prevented' here translates 'praeveniri' which means 'are started', 'set going'.
[17] *ibid.* p. 78.
[18] *ibid.* p. 79.
[19] *ibid.* p 81.
[20] *ibid.* p. 79.
[21] *ibid.* p. 82.
[22] *ibid.* p. 79.

Many would disagree with St Augustine however in so far as he lets the divine power overshadow the human will so completely. It is on this score that Professor H. D. Lewis made such a trenchant criticism of Karl Barth's theology in the book *Morals and the New Theology*. It should however be remembered that St Augustine is thinking mainly of Christian moral standards and the special Christian quality of goodness. Speaking of the person who received divine aid—the power of the Holy Spirit—St Augustine says, 'there arises in his heart a delight in and a love of that supreme and unchangeable Good which is God'.[23] What contrasts with this is not moral wrongdoing, but *sin*: 'he who partakes of God has received from him the inability to sin'.[24] St Augustine is obviously working within the framework of Christian categories which are not simply moral goodness and moral wrongdoing, but Godly Goodness and sin. Most Christian believers would agree with St Augustine that the special quality of Christian goodness cannot be achieved without divine aid, though many would possibly want to make reservations as to the possibility of there being a certain secular standard of moral goodness which is attainable without divine assistance.

The position might be somewhat clarified if more attention were paid to a distinction which is present in St Augustine's writings, namely, that between freedom of choice and perseverance. He seems to think that the divine power both makes us choose the Godly righteousness *and* enables us to persevere in its pursuit, but the first part of his contention is certainly much more questionable than the second. We are immediately up against some serious difficulties if we maintain that God compels us to choose what is good, but it seems to me quite plausible to hold that divine power is supporting our perseverance in all cases of moral achievements, and it is this latter contention that is the more closely relevant to our discussion here. When we talk of will-power, as distinct from freedom of the will, we are thinking more of the perseverance aspect of it, we are thinking more of the actual doing of things, the carrying through of our projects and plans.

[23] *Documents of the Christian Church* p. 77.
[24] *ibid.* p. 81.

So far as perseverance is concerned it seems to me that St Augustine's claim is a consistent one which most Christians would want to make. Most Christian believers would want to hold that there is a divine power involved in every case of moral perseverance and achievement where the moral standard in question is the special Christian one. I shall have more to say in a subsequent chapter about the difference between moral goodness and the goodness that is associated with, and sometimes even called, holiness.

To sum up, the power of holiness is typically manifested in situations where a very special aim is set to be achieved. That aim is to live the life of 'Godly Goodness'—an aim which cannot be achieved in the strength of our own will-power and which is only achieved at all in so far as a stronger will-power sustains us and carries us through to victory. Thus it is a situation in which it is correct to speak of will-power only if it is realized that the will-power in question is extraordinary. What sort of will-power can it be? Since will-power is something that is distinctively personal, then this extraordinary will-power must belong to an extraordinary 'person', and it appears that only by getting clearer about what we mean by such a 'person' that our question will be properly answered.

What goes for the term 'will-power' goes for the word 'life' too in this connection. The power of holiness may be spoken of in terms of 'life' so long as life is seen as something more than a mere complex of observable changes. Thus in both these terms—'will-power' and 'life'—we have logical stepping-stones by which we can make the crossing from a down-to-earth account of certain situations in terms of their observable features to an account of those situations in terms of holiness. Anyone who is convinced that there are situations where a more-than-human will-power is manifest, or that there is more to life than the biologist can account for, is also in a position to grasp what Hebrews and Christians have meant by the 'power' of holiness.

The mention of will-power reminds us of another power which is comparable to it in some ways, and which has moreover been associated with holiness. This is the power of love. Like will-power, it has to do with observable behaviour but also, like will-power, it is not entirely tractable in observational terms. Furthermore, both powers are highly personal, and both are more often than not associated with situations in which special effort and sacrifice are involved. St Thomas Aquinas points out that if a certain good that is to be achieved is of a particularly high standard then will-power must be superseded by the power of love—'if an object universally and in every respect good is proposed, then of necessity the will must go out in love if it acts at all'.[25] Thus, if a discussion of will-power can help us to understand what is meant by 'power of holiness', a discussion of the power of love should prove still more helpful.

THE POWER OF LOVE

To do good, in the Christian sense, certainly involves loving our fellowmen. It is not surprising therefore that the power of the Holy Spirit has also been thought of as a power of love. In Romans 5/5 we read: 'the love of God is shed abroad in our hearts by the Holy Ghost, which is given unto us'. C. H. Dodd interprets St Paul's teaching thus: 'Paul was immediately aware that when he was in close touch with Christ, that divine energy or power which he recognized as the spirit was released within him; and conversely, the full moral effect of that power was realized only through reference to Christ as revealing the eternal Love.'[26] Again, Evelyn Underhill quotes Eckhart as saying: 'all those motives by which we are moved to love, in these is nothing else than the Holy Spirit'.[27] It is not only that the power of the Holy Spirit causes love, and loving behaviour, but it is itself called 'love'. As Bethune-Baker reminds us, St Augustine believed that: 'the Holy Spirit may thus be specially called love'.[28] And as an example of a modern religious thinker who believes precisely the same thing we can quote H. H. Farmer who says: 'the divine energy and life are to be conceived in

[25] *St Thomas Aquinas: Philosophical Texts* p. 262. (Oxford, 1956).
[26] *Romans* (Dodd) p. 124.
[27] *Mysticism* p. 117. (Methuen, 1930).
[28] *Introduction to the Early History of Christian Doctrine* p. 230.

terms of the most personal of all categories, namely *agape* or love'.[29]

Thus 'love' has been accepted as an alternative description for holy power, but we have to tread carefully here, for we should notice that in our references to St Paul's teaching the love he mentions is the 'love of *God*', and in C. H. Dodd's interpretative passage it is of 'eternal love' that he speaks. Before considering the force of these qualifications however it may be as well to consider more ordinary love-situations first.

As good a love-situation as any to begin with would be that in which two young people are courting. We say that they are 'in love' or that they 'love' each other. Some people might want to hold that all this means is that the youngsters are sexually attracted by each other, or that they are expressing their sexual urge. The word 'love' is often used to refer to nothing more than what is an expression of the sexual urge. But the same word is often used in a very different sense too, even in this context. If someone could convince us that a certain young couple do not really have much to say to each other, that their life interests are very different, and that the *only* reason for their courtship is a sexual appeal, then we might well say: 'they are not really in love then; they do not really love each other', or we might say 'it is only a case of calf-love then'—the point being that we want to distinguish this from another meaning of 'love'. Again, others would describe mere sexual attraction as being a *baser* form of love, or they might refuse to use the word 'love' at all for such a relationship and maintain that it is only a case of animal instincts and nothing else. Undoubtedly, the word 'love' is more often than not used in a situation which is not exhaustively described in terms of animal instincts or sexual urge. Those elements may be present too but there is also more.

The meaning of 'love' can be still further drawn out if we consider a rather different example. There is a love relationship within the family circle which is not so closely related to sex as that between husband and wife. Take the case of a child's love for its parents. This might indeed be given a neat unpacking in terms of need for protection, dependence and so forth.

[29] *Revelation and Religion* p. 186.

Much of this observational aspect of the child's love is, however, to be found in the relationship of young animals to the mother parent, but we would not say that the little lamb *loves* its mother. The child's love for its parents does include this aspect of its behaviour but the love is not simply that in itself. There are cases of children ceasing to worry about their parents' welfare once they themselves have acquired their independence and we should say of such children, not simply that they have ceased to love their parents, but that they never really loved them at all. So-called loving behaviour towards parents which is simply for the sake of their protection, because they give us the only security we know and so on, is, in a sense, quite unworthy of the word 'love'. If a child behaved kindly towards its parents *as its* parents, *because* they happen to be *its* parents, then there is some sense in holding that this is not true love. Or consider the reverse relationship. If a father loves his child simply as *his* child, then there might be some point in claiming that this is not really love, or that it is not love in its fullest sense. Suppose a father suddenly realized that one of the children reared on his hearth is not really his own child after all. Admittedly the situation would be a very complicated one, and would involve many factors such as shock, a sense of having been deceived, and so on, which would account in part for the father's change of attitude to this particular unfortunate child. However, allowing for all this, one could reasonably hold that if the father really *loved* the child in the first place this sudden discovery should make no appreciable difference to his behaviour towards the child. Even a subtle difference in the father's subsequent behaviour would tend to suggest that his previous behaviour could be better explained without bringing in the word 'love'. We might prefer to explain this former behaviour in terms of parental instinct which naturally lost force when the father realized that he was not the father of *this* child.

Within the family circle there is an interplay of sexual impulse, need for protection, parental instinct, and this in a way explains much of the behaviour of the members of a family. But if it were conceded that the whole love-like behaviour of a particular family was such that it could be accounted for *entirely* in this way we should want to say that there was no real love-relationship existing there. It seems to me that part of the force of the word *'love'* is to deny that family relationship could be explained entirely in terms of instincts and impulses.

This 'love' which is more than sexual impulse or parental instinct is most clearly evident in those cases where such impulses and instincts are absent. We can imagine cases where the loving person's behaviour was not at all explicable in terms of instincts or impulses. Take the case where a man loves his enemy for instance. The enemy's behaviour may be vile, yet the other man persists in responding kindly and considerately. Admittedly, the public behaviour pattern of love need not be homogeneous, for love may be expressed in chastisement (Cf. 'whom the Lord loveth he chasteneth' Heb. 12/6). The important point is however that here we have a situation where biological or even psychological explanations prove inadequate. The psychologist may show remarkable ingenuity in tracing what appears as altruistic behaviour to hidden selfish desires in some cases, but he would certainly be defeating his own end if he insisted that *all* apparently altruistic action can be explained in that way. Altruism is not in principle impossible, and it is in such a connection that one would speak of sheer, selfless love. This case of purely altruistic behaviour is indeed an extreme one where all biological and psychological explanations of the situation are clearly least adequate but this does not mean that 'love' in the same sense may not also be present on the hearth, in the home, and where betrothed meet. What I have tried to emphasize is that the word 'love' usually points to an 'extra' which cannot be easily and completely unpacked in terms of observational behaviour.

It is when the word 'love' is taken in the above sense that we are brought nearest to what is meant by the 'love' which is also holy power. If we are to understand what 'love' in this special sense means then the meaning of human love even at its highest must be stretched beyond all present conceptions. The love which is holy power is love *eternal* and this implies that it reaches out to all mankind in all ages and persists whatever the extent and nature of enmity shown. The situation ceases to be one which we can straightforwardly describe. In considering what can be meant by 'love' when the words 'of God' are added we immediately think of St John's words 'for God so loved the world that he gave his only begotten Son, that whosoever believeth in him should not perish, but have eternal life'.[30] This directs our attention to the person and life of Christ. We have to realize *what* he sacrificed for our sakes, and *what* he gave to us. He abandoned the life *eternal* that we might enjoy life *eternal*, becoming what we are that we might become what he is.[31] As Farmer said—love is the 'most *personal* of all categories', and to know the love which is the power of holiness is also to know a person, though as I have said before he is an unique 'person'.

Let me explain further how the personal element comes into any proper understanding of love. Think of some of the reasons that may be given for the love shown towards a particular person. Some of the reasons may be difficult to explain, but others will be fairly straightforward. Examples of these answers would be (a) 'because she is beautiful', 'because he is kind', 'because they have sacrificed so much for me', (b) 'because she is Stella, 'because he is John', 'because he is my son', 'because they are my parents'. In the first type of answer we see that very much depends upon the person loved having certain qualities which we would all agree to be some of the things that might make a person lovable to us. If these answers were exhaustive then we know quite well what would have to be different for the particular love in question to be absent, and this would depend very much more upon the object of love than upon the lover himself. We should also tend to say that the love for which these reasons were given was rather superficial, unless of course it was specifically pointed out that such reasons only give a small part of the story. If such reasons as these are exhaustive, then we should class that love with the kind of thing we sometimes call 'cupboard-love'.

The second class of reasons are rather different. It must be admitted in the first place of course that even here the type of answer given in (a) would not be irrelevant. Though beauty,

[30] John 3/16.
[31] Cf. Athanasius in *De Incarnatione* 54-3. (Nutt, 1885).

kindness and sacrifice are not everything in this second case, still it can be conceded even here that matters might be somewhat different if these desirable qualities and factors were absent. If a wife loves her husband just because he is the person he is, because he is John, then true enough she does not love him simply and only for his kindness, nevertheless this does not imply that her love would not be different if John was not kind. It is obvious that in this second case also much depends upon the object of the love being what he or she is.

This does not however complete the story. When someone says that he or she loves a person for what that person is, for 'himself', there may be much more to this contention than what I have just said. Consider a case where John ceased to be kind, and loses many characteristics which Stella used to admire in him. She might still continue to love him, and if challenged about keeping her affection for such a disappointing character she might explain: 'but he is still John isn't he?' We might retort that she is a fool to love him any longer, but she need not concede that she is foolish if she modifies her behaviour towards John while still maintaining that she loves him. Love is not necessarily a matter of being slavish or silly; indeed it is the particular genius of true love that it can find an inexhaustible variety of behaviour patterns to cope with difficult situations. So we can imagine a woman still loving a worthless and degenerate husband despite the changes wrought in him.

This time however the love apparently depends much less upon its object and much more upon the lover herself. Yet the wife might still be able to bring forth some good reasons for saying that despite all change her husband is still the same John, though we can think of the wife's reasons for saying he is still the same John getting fewer and fewer, while the reasons that can be brought against her belief pile up higher and higher. Eventually a deadlock is reached at which there are as many reasons for saying that John is a completely different person as there are for holding otherwise.

If this wife still loves him at this point it is not the objective features of the situation that have decided the issue. We feel like turning round and saying that the wife herself decided the issue. The person in our example loves her husband simply

because she is who she is; to love in these particular circumstances is simply to be the person she is.

Thus love is a distinctively personal thing, and the power
of love is a personal power. Yet strangely enough, if we were
to ask Stella why she loves her husband, she would never admit
that it is because she is the person she happens to be; her
reason would be, on the contrary, that *John* is the person *he*
happens to be, and no matter how we argue, we can never
show that Stella is wrong and that John is not the person she
thinks he is. We are, it must be remembered, presupposing
that all the factual arguments have already been brought to the
fore, that Stella accepts the facts, but still sees John as the same
person and still loves him. It is no use trying to point out to her
that John only appears to her to be the same person because
she chooses to take a particular attitude to him, for the choice
and the attitude are simply an expression of her way of seeing
things in these particular circumstances, and that is the only
way she possibly can see them. She cannot be expected to see
John as though she herself were somebody other than Stella.
She simply *is* Stella, and to say that she sees John as Stella sees
him is simply to draw out the implication of that primary
assertion. We cannot prove that Stella is wrong; we can only
prove that Stella is not one of us and vice versa.

I have been trying to show that in some cases love is not a
merely rational response, but a personal one. This, it seems to
me, is the sort of response we more often than not have in mind
when we use the word 'love'. As was pointed out earlier, if a
clear, simple and exhaustive explanation of our love can be
given then we tend to withdraw the word 'love' in such cases,
or substitute for it such terms as 'cupboard-love' to denote its
superficiality. We are most happy to use the word 'love' un-
qualified when the lover *cannot* exhaustively explain himself
in rational terms. I think that most people would agree that this
last is a case of 'genuine' love, and the only explanation then
is that the people involved are what they are. Love is personal,
and if we think of love as a power, then it is a personal power;
or if we call a certain power 'love', then that power is personal.

If there is any force in what I have just argued, then one can
begin to see what Christian believers mean when they say that

the power of the holy spirit is love and that it is therefore a personal power. A. W. E. Blunt, in his commentary on the Acts, says of the 'holy spirit' that 'its meaning oscillates between a person and an influence',[32] and he adds a little later, 'the conception (i.e. of the holy spirit) in Acts trembles on the verge of ascribing personality to the Spirit'.[32] This tendency which was begun in Acts is, according to Blunt, 'carried further in Paul'.[32] Soon after the early doctrinal controversies of the early Christian Church began, it became evident that one of the major Christian contentions was that the holy spirit had a personal existence. For example, Bethune Baker reminds us that Cyril of Jerusalem refers to the holy spirit as 'living and personally subsisting and always present together with the Father and the Son'.[33] The power of holiness is a personal power; the holy situation is a situation of personal power.

To what extent does all this help us to understand what a situation of holy power is like? Take a situation where a human person shows love for another, then alter the picture so that there are no obvious reasons for any love being shown, and it becomes plain that the love in question is due to the lover being the person he is. Then take matters still further, and think of a person who loves his enemies, does good to them that harm him, and so forth. The story should be developed in this altruistic direction until a point is reached where we want to say that there is more to it than just a matter of this person being who he is. If the story is developed properly we shall begin by admiring the man who shows such genuine love, then we shall deeply respect him as his love is shown to extend further, and as the tale develops we shall feel a reverence for the man, then veneration, and we shall end up by adoring him. But we have our doubts about according adoration to a human being. We have reached a point at which we feel that something more is present than just a human being. There is strong reason to believe that the disciples' experience in the company of Jesus corresponded to the development of the story as I have just indicated. They ended up by adoring Jesus, calling him the Son of God, deifying him. Thus, for them, it became correct to use

[32] *Acts (Clarendon Bible)* p. 145. (Oxford, 1948).
[33] *Introduction to Early History of Christian Doctrine* p. 208.

the word 'God' in a situation in which Jesus was present. They reached a situation in their experience of Jesus when they felt that there was more present than just the man Jesus. To love as Jesus loved was to be the person he was, but it was not the same as to be no more than a particular human being. To love as Jesus did was to be a person about whom the disciples wanted to deny that he was simply a *human* person, though he was that as well. To say that Jesus loved as he did amounted not only to saying that he was who he was, but also to saying that he was divine. The holy spirit was the power of love—the love of *this* person—but this person was not simply a historical Jesus who died, but also a divine Christ who still lives.

A situation of holy power today would be one where we have a man showing this same power of love that would evoke in us a response similar to that evoked by Jesus Christ himself. It is to such a situation as this that Christians refer when they talk of a man as being in Christ, or of Christ as being in him. Such, presumably, should a holy man be.

This discussion leaves on our hands the question: what is meant by divine personality? It is, as I have hinted before, a crucial one for the proper understanding of what holiness means. Before we can proceed to discuss it however, I must turn to another aspect of holiness where it seems to imply wholeness.

CHAPTER VI

HOLINESS OR WHOLENESS?

THE word 'whole' or 'wholeness', in virtue of its etymological affinity with the word 'holiness' deserves to be considered as a possible logical kinsman of the latter. It seems to me that 'wholeness' understood in a special sense, could be used as a substitute for 'holiness' in many contexts, and in the present chapter I shall try to substantiate that claim. In doing so I shall also have to make clear as far as is possible what is the special sense of 'wholeness' that I have in mind. There is, admittedly, some uncertainty as to the primitive pre-Christian meaning of 'hailo' from which the word 'holy' derives but the Oxford English Dictionary goes so far as to say that 'it is with some probability assumed to have been "inviolate, inviolable, that must be preserved *whole* or intact, that cannot be injured with impunity".' The ultimate root is 'hāl' from which the word 'whole' itself derives, and it is worth remembering that the word 'health' comes from the same root. We shall see in due course that 'holiness' is also closely associated with 'health' in the Old Testament as well as the New Testament. In the *Hasting's Dictionary of the Bible*, G. B. Stevens tells us that ἅγιος, which expresses the characteristic New Testament idea of holiness, means Godlikeness and that 'in the Christian system Godlikeness signifies *completeness* of life'.[1] This amounts to saying that 'ἅγιος', 'Godlikeness' and 'completeness of life' are logical equivalents, and what interests us in the present context is that the idea of wholeness appears in the last of these terms. Thus, if we can find out more about the special kind of completeness or 'wholeness' involved here, some light should thereby be thrown upon the logic of 'holiness' too.

I must at the outset however mention one point which complicates matters considerably. Holiness often implies separation. In the very article by Stevens, from which I quoted above, we

[1] *Hasting's Dictionary of the Bible* Vol. II p. 400a. (My italics).

also read: 'it is generally believed that the fundamental idea which underlies the word is that of separation'.[2] Stevens is not unduly worried by the contrast between separatedness and completeness which are both implied by ἄγιος for he seems to regard them as being two sides of the same coin. He regards holiness as implying 'separation from sin, and so, consecration to God'.[2] Thus to participate in the 'wholeness' or completeness which we are about to consider is at the same time to be separate from anything which is not incorporated into that same 'whole' or 'unity'. It is true of course that unity often does imply separation; to be united with the allies, for instance, implies being separate from the enemy. One might contend that it is the same in religion. E. F. Scott says, with reference to the consecration of the disciples, that they 'have part in the higher life, and are not of the world'.[3] It seems that to participate in the higher life implies separation from the 'world'. Special problems will arise however if we want to maintain that the special unity, or complete 'whole' which is holiness is all-embracing or in some sense absolute. This question of separation will have to be given a more extensive treatment after I have entered more fully into a discussion of the 'wholeness' or 'unity' to which I want to give immediate attention.

My discussion in this chapter will fall into three sections in which I wish to consider different, but inter-related, ways of understanding the wholeness which is holiness. The three approaches start off with references in the respective cases to (a) the Hebrew conception of property, (b) holy vocation and holy sacrifice and (c) holiness and cleanliness.

PROPERTY

I think some light can be thrown on the special kind of wholeness which is also holiness by an investigation into the Hebrew concept of property. This is doubly worth while in view of the fact that the holy is also invariably that which *belongs* to God, whatever that may mean. The Hebrews cer-

---

[2] *Hasting's Dictionary of the Bible* Vol. II p. 399b.
[3] *The Literature of the New Testament—The Fourth Gospel* p. 226. (T. & T. Clarke, 1908).

tainly thought of that which was holy as being the property of their God, and everything that was given to God became holy thereby. 'Cattle, or objects, are made holy by giving them to Yahweh (Lev. 27/9).'[4] 'To set something apart as the possession of Yahweh's is to consecrate or sanctify it (קָדֵשׁ) (see Judges 17/3, II Sam. 8/11, I Kings 7/51, 15/15).'[4] Holy bread belongs to God: 'he shall eat the bread of his God, both of the most holy, and of the holy' (Lev. 21/22). It is no accident that the possessive adjective so often comes in apposition to the word 'holy': 'my holy name' (Lev. 20/3), 'his holy arm' (Is. 52/10), 'his holy word' (Ps. 105/42), and 'his holy spirit' (Is. 63/10. In Ex. 19/12f. we read of Moses being commanded to set bounds for the people so that they should not trespass upon the holy mount Sinai, 'or touch the border of it'. The land beyond the boundary was not the property of the people of Israel but, so it seems, the special property of God. Whatever we think of the historical truth of the mount Sinai incidents, we must agree that mountains and high places were always connected with holiness in Jewish thought and whenever reference is made to a holy mountain there is an indication that it is the property of God: 'they shall not hurt nor destroy in all *my* holy mountain' (Is. 65/25), 'for in *mine* holy mountain . . ." (Ex. 20/40), '*thy* holy mountain' (Dan. 9/16).[5]

Such language is personal and the God whose property holy things are is obviously thought of as being a person, though what kind of person remains to be seen. It will suffice for the present if we bear in mind that he is no ordinary person. But how far does this take us towards understanding what is that 'wholeness' which is holiness? It takes us nowhere if we think in terms of one common, present-day meaning of the word 'property'. We often think of property in terms of purchasing and selling price, title-deeds, rights of use and so forth, but this does not take us any distance in our understanding of the holy as being owned by God, for he did not pay a price for his holy mount nor is it ear-marked with a selling price, and there are no title-deeds which we could inspect. God never occupies his property or resides therein in the same way as an ordinary

---

[4] *The Prophetical Conception of Holiness* p. 11.
[5] My italics. Cf. also Is. 56/7, 11/9, 57/13, 65/11, and Joel 2/1.

house-owner occupies his house and resides there.

Some light is thrown on our problem, however, once we turn to the Hebrew conception of property. The Hebrews thought of a man's property as being in some sense an extension of his personality. 'All that man possesses and that belongs to his sphere is penetrated by his soul; . . . this holds good of his tools, his house, his animals, the whole of his property.'[6] This Hebrew conception of property is well emphasized by Aubrey R. Johnson (now Professor Johnson) in his monograph entitled *The One and the Many in the Israelite Conception of God*. He gives various examples which show that 'any part of a man's property is thought to form an "extension" of the personality';[7] he shows how even the 'spoken word may be regarded as an effective "extension" of the personality',[8] and 'in the same way the "Name" is an important "Extension" of Yahweh's Personality'.[9] This idea of property as being an extension of personality should not be incomprehensible to us today for we know of something very like this in our own lives. Of course we hardly think of a person's property as possessing a magical power belonging to the person, as Gehazi, the bearer of Elisha's staff, was taught to believe. In so far as the Hebrews thought of this extension as being such a quasi-physical power their views would be considered outmoded and superstitious today.

We do however often treat certain objects as though they were intimately related with another person. Consider the gifts we receive from other people for instance. They often have a value for us which is far in excess of their worth in money, and to which the latter is irrelevant; it is what we call sentimental value. This is why a book which has the well-known author's autograph on it can be much more valuable than an ordinary copy. If we respect the person connected with these objects of sentimental value then we still feel that the objects are in some sense 'his' or 'hers'; we do not feel very happy about selling them for instance, and in extreme cases we feel disinclined to use them even. Such objects are respected and preserved as

[6] *Israel* I and II. p. 170.
[7] *The One and the Many in the Israelite Conception of God* p. 10 (University of Wales Press, 1942).
[8] ibid. p. 6.   [9] ibid. p. 21.

though they were some sort of 'extension' of the person we connect with them. A similar view of the relation of objects to persons holds when we disrespect them. As effective a way as any of insulting someone is to maltreat something which belongs to him—to kick his dog for instance, or to smash the vase he or she once gave us as a present. And we can all understand the satisfaction which the irreverent boy found by catapulting peas at the photograph of a relative whom he particularly disliked.

The matter might be made still clearer if we think of a person's relation to his own body. We often speak of the body as though it were a property which the person owns; we speak of '*my* arms, legs, eyes', or '*my* body', and if pressed on the question we certainly want to hold on to the distinction here implied between a person and his body. Few would concede that a person *is* his body. Yet, such is the intimacy of the relation of a person to his body that we would hold that any maltreatment of a person's body amounts to an assault upon, and an insult to, the person himself.

At this point it is possible to begin a more constructive account of the matter. A person's body, while not in itself constituting the unity or wholeness of the person, is nevertheless something observable and tangible which we almost invariably associate with the whole person. The body of a person participates in the whole which is more than the aggregate of the observables involved, and which is the person himself. It is in virtue of this fact that we can point to a person's living body and say 'that is John' or 'that is Mary', yet with the intention, *not* of referring to the person's body as such, but to the whole person.

But a person's body is not the only belonging which we think of as somehow intimately connected with his whole person. Certain objects which a person uses, possesses, or made perhaps, become inextricably bound up with the totality of his personality in our minds, so that we hardly even think of them without thinking of him too. And this is also true of the members of his family, a man's wife and children. We still speak of children 'doing their parents credit' as though they were in a sense 'extensions' of the personality of the parents. Such are the diverse manifestations of a single person. It is in this light that we can make sense of the Hebrew idea that a man's property and family were 'extensions' of his personality. What belongs to a man participates in a unity which is the wholeness of his person.

It is in a similar light that we can understand the Hebrew view of God's property as being holy. What belongs to God participates in his wholeness which is a personal wholeness. As a person's body or personal belongings or family become inextricably bound up with the person himself in the unity of his personality so also do the things, and the people, that belong to God become bound up in a unity with his person. Thus when the ark of the Lord, for example, came into the Israelite camp, the Philistines were to understand that 'God' had 'come into the camp' (I Sam. 4/5-8), so that the respect owing to God should be paid to the ark as well. The ark was nothing in itself that it should cause so much concern, but when it was thought of as belonging to the 'wholeness' of God it demanded a reaction that would only be appropriate when a person was present, and a very exceptional person at that.

Many instances of Hebrew prohibitions which seem pointless to us today take on a new significance if understood in the light of what I have just said. Take the prohibition in Ex. 19/12 which reads 'and thou shalt set bounds unto the people round about, saying, Take heed to yourselves, that ye go not up into the mount, or touch the border of it: whosoever toucheth the mount shall surely be put to death'. If all that were involved here were the relation of a people to a piece of ground on the side of a mountain, then one might well ask : 'What is all the fuss about?' But if these people thought of the mountain as belonging to, and incorporated in, a 'whole' which was 'personal', yet not like any ordinary person, then we can well understand the Hebrews' trepidation and caution. In the same way, we can also understand the attitude of Christians in our own day when they show exceptional respect to what outwardly appears to be nothing but another building in the parish. Present-day Christians think of their local church buildings as being 'God's house', and they still associate God's house with his person in such a way as to pay to the church the respects expressive of their attitude to God. The church is a building set apart, and though it might be suitable for holding all sorts of functions, all except those of a worshipful character are kept out of it. It belongs to God, not to the parish, and to disrespect it would be to insult God himself.

We should always remember that to call a thing, or a building, or a place 'holy', is not to say that any of these things are themselves wholes, but that they belong to a greater 'whole', an extraordinary personal whole, that is, God. Objects and places may have an unity or wholeness of their own, but the word 'holy' does not refer to that. It refers to the 'unity' and 'wholeness' of God—not of course that I have explained what this extraordinary 'wholeness' is by any means. To say that it is personal is however something, and that can serve as a basis for a fuller discussion later on.

People, as well as things and places, can be holy, and the holiness of people can also be better understood as participation in the exceptional 'wholeness' which we are discussing. I have already hinted at the fact that the Hebrew thought of a person as being extended into his family : 'the household in its entirety is regarded as a psychical whole—the extended personality of the man at its head'.[10] Holy people are people who belong to God's family. George Johnston, expounding St Paul's teaching on the Church says: 'as Yahweh was the Father of Israel, so God was known as the Father of Jesus Christ: in Christ the Christian community discovered its sonship and its family relationships. God's people were God's family, members of the household of faith.'[11] The same idea—that being holy involves belonging to God's family—is present in Eph. 1/4-5: 'that we should be holy and without blemish before him in love: having foreordained us unto adoption as *sons* . . .' (my italics).

Now, just as the Hebrew thought of the person of the head of a family as being extended into the whole family, so did he think of God, the head of the family of people that belong to him, as being extended into them. That is, the holy man was

[10] *The One and the Many in the Israelite Conception of God* p.8.
[11] *The Doctrine of the Church in the New Testament* p. 79. (Cambridge, 1943).

thought to participate in the wholeness of God. This was especially so in the case of the prophet—one of the most holy amongst them. 'The prophet', says Aubrey R. Johnson, 'in functioning, was held to be more than Yahweh's "representative", for the time being he was an active "Extension" of Yahweh's Personality and, as such, *was* Yahweh—"in Person".'[12] Thus to say that a man was holy would be to say that he belonged to a whole, which is greater than himself, a whole that was 'personal', yet not precisely as the man himself was personal. The word 'family' when used of the unity of God and his people is not used in its ordinary sense. This unity is a 'family' in a special sense of that word. The 'family' of God is a group of people who belong together in virtue of a common participation in this 'whole' which is greater than the individuals included in it. Thus it should not surprise us to find that Oscar Cullman detects in the New Testament (I Cor. 7/14) the 'idea of a family solidarity in holiness'.[13] Cullman says that holiness is *the fact of belonging to the "saints"*.'[13] This definition may be accepted provided we interpret it as meaning 'the fact of being one of those into whom God's personality is extended'. The important point is that this 'family' is only such in virtue of what God is, and of the fact that he has incorporated these people into himself. This he does according to Pauline teaching through Christ, so that it can be said of these people that they are the 'body of Christ' (I. Cor. 12/27). Just as an ordinary person is extended into his body so the divine Christ who is one with the Father (the head of the family) is extended into the family of God, the Church, the New Israel.

It is only in virtue of this special relationship with God that the Israelites of the Old Testament period, even, could look upon themselves as a holy people. They were a *chosen* holy people (Deut 7/6), and the same is true of the New Israel. As Johnston says: 'to be truly Israel means to belong to God; to be a people *only by his favour and choice*'.[14] It is not Israel's own choice, or any of her actions, that makes her holy, but the fact that she was chosen by God. This word 'choosing' is again

---

[12] *The One and the Many in the Israelite Conception of God* p. 37.
[13] *Baptism in the New Testament* p. 53. (S.C.M. Press, 1950).
[14] *The Doctrine of the Church in the New Testament* p. 85. (My italics).

a way of expressing God's incorporation of these people into the 'wholeness' of his own personality. The nearest possible parallel to this in ordinary Hebrew life would perhaps be the case where a man chooses his wife, and she thereby participates in the wholeness of his personality.

HOLY VOCATION AND HOLY SACRIFICE

Holiness is still seen to involve union with a divine personal whole when we consider the fact that holy people are not infrequently identified as the people with a special vocation which separates them from ordinary folk. Holy men were men set apart for certain special tasks such as ministering at the altar in Old Testament religion (see Ex. 29/1ff where the details are given of how a person is to be consecrated for the priest's office), or serving king and country on a campaign (see I Sam. 21/5,6 where the young soldiers are considered holy enough to appropriate the holy bread). Service of God and holiness are also connected in New Testament teaching for, as Vincent Taylor points out, 'the reconciling work of God . . . is itself a sanctifying activity, in the sense that the believer is set apart and consecrated to holy ends and purposes'.[15] But this service is also not only a matter of performing rites and ceremonies but of commitment to a certain way of life. Johnston emphasizes that to be truly Israel meant to belong to God, 'to have no lesser function than to serve the living God'.[16] Here, holy people are those who serve holy ends and purposes. Their behaviour is therefore not to be interpreted in the light of their own personal ends and purposes only, but rather in the light of the ends and purposes of God. Their behaviour should be an expression of the purposes of God, and in so far as a purpose reflects the person who possesses it, the behaviour of holy people should reflect God's person.[17] Once again the idea that a holy person participates in a personal unity which is more than himself becomes unavoidable.

[15] *Forgiveness and Reconciliation* p. 444. (Macmillan, 1948).
[16] *The Doctrine of the Church in the New Testament* p. 85.
[17] This is in keeping with the Hebrew view of prophecy for instance. When the prophet is speaking God's word, no sharp distinction is drawn between God and the prophet, and the latter often speaks in the first person when uttering God's message. (e.g. Is. Ch. 56).

The view that holiness amounts to participation in the wholeness of the divine personality fits in well with the Hebrew and Christian views about sacrifice. There are two different interpretations of Hebrew sacrifice which I would like to consider, both of which point eventually in the same direction. The first is that put forward by W. Robertson Smith in his book *The Religion of the Semites*. He holds that 'the leading idea in the animal sacrifices of the Semites . . . was not that of a gift made over to the god, but an act of communion, in which the god and his worshippers unite by partaking together of the flesh and blood of a sacred victim'.[18] Later in the same book he writes: 'the one point that comes out clear and strong is that the fundamental idea of ancient sacrifice is sacramental communion, and that all atoning rites are ultimately to be regarded as owing their efficacy to a communication of divine life to the worshippers, and to the establishment or confirmation of a living bond between them and their god'.[19] Sacrifice constituted an important part of the Hebrew cultus, and one of the objects of the cult ceremonies was, to quote Ringgren, 'to put oneself in the state of holiness that is required by the holy act'.[20] Thus to put oneself in a state of holiness amounted, on Robertson Smith's interpretation of sacrifice, to coming into a union with God such that one partook of his life. This is very much in line with what I have been arguing above, namely, that the holiness of a human person involves participating in the divine personal 'whole' which is God.

A different interpretation of sacrifice is adopted by G. B. Gray, but this leads eventually to a very similar conclusion. Gray, speaking of the movement of Old Testament religion upward towards a spiritual goal, says: 'it rises to the conception that there is . . . a gift of something that is his (man's) own and that God desires to receive; man can give himself; his will is his own, he can make it his present to God'.[21] Here again the dominating idea is that man through sacrifice seeks union with God; the offering of gifts stands for something more—the

---

[18] *The Religion of the Semites* p. 226-227. (Black, 1927).
[19] ibid. p. 439.
[20] *The Prophetical Conception of Holiness* p. 10.
[21] *Sacrifice in the Old Testament* p. 54. (Clarendon, 1925).

offering of man himself to be incorporated into the unity of God. Vincent Taylor lends some support to this view when he says that 'we are far from idealizing unduly the Old Testament sacrificial system if we assert that for many worshippers it was the vehicle of a truly spiritual approach to God and an opportunity for self-offering and surrender'.[22]

The same idea is prominent in the New Testament. We remember St Paul's injunction to self-sacrifice: 'I beseech you therefore, brethren, by the mercies of God, to present your bodies a living sacrifice, holy, acceptable to God which is your reasonable service' (Romans 12/1). 'The body' in St Paul's writings means more than the flesh; it means the whole personality.[23] Since his incarnation, life and death on the cross Christ himself has taken the place of the sacrificial beast and it is through his sacrifice that we now come into communion with God. As J. Scott Lidgett says: 'we become one with Him in His submission and self-oblation; one with Him, also, in His high-priestly acts'.[24] Thinkers who specially emphasize this unity with Christ which atonement involves often refer back to the etymological origin of the word—'at-one-ment',[25] and certainly few would deny that the main purpose of Christ's life and death was to bring men into union with himself and God. Moreover, this act of incorporating people into an unity with God in himself is Christ's *sanctification* of his people. In the well-known seventeenth chapter of St John's Gospel we read: 'and for their sakes I *sanctify* myself, that they themselves also may be *sanctified* in truth' (John 17/19), and a little later 'that they may all be *one*; even as thou, Father, art in me, and I in thee, that they also may be in us' (John 17/21). The author of the Epistle to the Hebrews puts it succinctly, and in true Johannine tradition, when he says 'for both he that sanctifieth and they that are sanctified are all of one'. (Heb. 2/11).

In this latter context the unity is also pictured as a family, for the author immediately adds 'for which cause he is not ashamed to call them brethren' (Heb. 2/11)—brethren not in

---

[22] *Jesus and His Sacrifice* p. 59. (Macmillan, 1951).
[23] *Romans* (Dodd) p. 90.
[24] *The Spiritual Principle of the Atonement* p. 408. (R. Culley, 1897).
[25] See *The Atonement* by T. H. Hughes p. 232. (Allen & Unwin, 1949).

virtue of an ordinary blood kinship,[26] but in virtue of an extraordinary bond of unity. They are 'holy brethren' (Heb. 3/1),
brethren through this family bond which is more than an
ordinary family bond. Holy brethren are united in, and through
the person who sanctifies them, Jesus Christ. They become one
with him, and if we ask 'How?', then the answer is 'in the same
way as he is united with his Father'. We are still speaking in
family terms, but it is no ordinary father and son that is meant
here, for though they are often spoken of as being two persons
yet they are *one*. What sort of unity is this? If God is a 'person'
at all, what kind of person is he? How are we to speak of him
at all? or to put it another way, what is the logic of the word
'person' when used of God? These are the questions that are
being forced once more to our notice.

HOLINESS AND CLEANNESS

I now want to see what light can be thrown on this 'unity'
or 'wholeness' by considering holiness as contrasted with uncleanness and impurity. I begin by quoting John Calvin, who
writes thus in his *Institutes*: 'when mention is made of our
union with God, let us remember that holiness must be the
bond . . . because it greatly concerns his glory not to have
any fellowship with wickedness and impurity'.[27] Calvin obviously thinks of holiness as being an uniting principle, and this
is in accordance with the view which I have elaborated above,
but he also thinks of this uniting principle as being something
that contrasts with wickedness and impurity. How is it to be
understood by contrast with these?

Much is made of the contrast between holiness and impurity
in the Old Testament. There, holiness is closely associated with
cleanness and is taken to be incompatible with uncleanness.
Indeed it often appears that holiness simply is cleanness. Part

[26] A discussion here of the significance of the word 'blood' in the sacrificial
context would take us too far afield, for there is considerable disagreement
between scholars on the matter. Behm in his article on $\alpha \tilde{\iota} \mu \alpha$ in Kittel's
Theologisches Wöterbuch (i pp. 171-5) holds that 'blood' signifies 'death'
whereas Vincent Taylor, for instance, argues that it means 'life released'. See
The Atonement in N.T. Teaching. (Epworth, 1940).

[27] *Institutes* Vol. II p. 3. (T. & T. Clarke, 1949).

of the instruction given to Aaron according to Lev. 10/10 was 'that ye may put difference between the holy and the common, and between the unclean and the clean'. Sacrificial animals had to be clean (Gen. 8/20), and anyone afflicted with uncleanness was debarred from ministering in the cult. Moreover, ' "to sanctify oneself" and "to purify or cleanse oneself" (יִטַּהֲרוּ) may sometimes be used as synonyms'.[28] It is also significant as Ringgren notes, that 'the Septuagint sometimes translates קדש with καθαρος, καθαριζειν or the like'.[29]

Still it would be wrong to conclude that holiness simply means cleanness in the ordinary sense of that word, for we find that many things that were in no sense unclean were not regarded as holy. Common bread was not unclean, yet it was not holy like the shewbread. The common grain used for ordinary consumption was not unclean, yet it was not holy like the first-fruit that was consecrated to God. Obviously 'clean' was not synonymous with 'holy', and I would suggest that such things as shewbread and the first-fruits were considered holy because they were given to God to be his and to be associated with the wholeness of his personality along the lines I have suggested above. But it is nonetheless significant that only clean things, and certainly not unclean things, could ever come to be holy at all. It was not just anything that could be offered to God; not everything would be acceptable to him, and if we take 'possession' to imply 'extension' of personality this meant that God's personality would not be extended into anything and everything indiscriminately. It was not anything and everything that could be integrated into the wholeness of God's personality, but only those which have special qualifications. For example, an unclean or maimed sacrificial animal would not do whereas a clean and healthy one would be quite acceptable.

Now, however much in the dark we may be as regards knowing what is meant by this mysterious 'wholeness' which is holiness, it is significant that the Hebrews thought that some things could be related to it in a way others could not. Even though it was not cleanness itself that made things holy, yet we

[28] *The Prophetical Conception of Holiness* p. 18.
[29] ibid. p. 18.

should not overlook the fact that this 'wholeness' is specially associated with clean things in a way it is not associated with others. It was not only the Hebrew who thought thus about holiness; we have often heard it said in our own day that 'cleanliness is next to Godliness' which suggests that many people today still think that, whatever the extraordinary personal unity known as God is like, it harmonizes with cleanliness in a way it does not harmonize with filth and dirt.

Cleanness in Hebrew thought involved more than washing of hands and garments. Let us look at some of the rules relating to this subject. The Nazarite would lose his holiness and become unclean if he touched a corpse (Num. 6/6). Similar effects followed if any Israelite touched or ate the carcass of dead animals (Lev. 11/24/25 and 39). If a person had an issue from his or her body then he or she automatically became unclean (Lev. 15/16, 19, 25). A woman with child was unclean for seven days (Lev. 12/2). The sufferer from leprosy was unclean throughout the period of his disease (Lev. Ch. 13 and 14). All this suggests that cleanness was associated with normal health whereas uncleanness was associated with ill-health, abnormality, and death. We should not conclude that holiness ever meant for the Hebrew 'healthiness' in the ordinary sense of that word, and nothing more. Conformity with the negative prohibitions just mentioned did not imply holiness; something more was required for that, namely, entrance into special relation with deity. But again, the fact that good health was an appropriate qualification for entry into such a relation is significant. Whatever the Hebrews thought about holiness—'divine personal wholeness' as I would suggest it might be alternatively called—it is evident that they believed that it was something with which health could harmonize in a way ill-health, abnormality and death could not.

One might fairly gather from the emphasis I have just laid on the significance of cleanness and health that they provide some clue to the nature of the 'divine whole' with which they seem so capable of intimate association. It might be thought that they are symbols of, or metaphors expressing, the 'divine whole', and if so, cannot we all readily think of something which those terms often do metaphorically represent, namely, moral goodness?

Admittedly, cleanness is often symbolic of moral goodness, witness our use of such expressions as, 'a clean record', 'clean living', 'I wash my hands of . . .' The word 'health' and its kinsmen can also be understood metaphorically. When we speak of a 'healthy' society we mean more than its physical wellbeing; there is a moral reference as well. Bodily defects such as blindness and lameness still provide useful symbols for moral weaknesses. Indeed, it may be plausibly argued that in Old Testament literature too cleanliness and its contrast symbolized moral goodness and its contrast. Sexual aberrations such as whoredom (Ezk. 23/17) and adultery (Lev. 18/20) rendered the people concerned unclean. The people who shed innocent blood were defiled thereby (Num. Ch. 35). Surely, one might argue, uncleanness here means moral weakness. In Is. 1/16 the emphasis has clearly shifted from the literal meaning of 'cleanness' to its symbolic, moral meaning. The prophet emphasizes that sacrifices and burnt offerings as such mean little to God; the cultic practices are depreciated as being of no value in themselves. Then the prophet begins his exhortation: 'wash you, make you clean' (Is. 1/16), and the following injunctions make it quite clear what this means, 'cease to do evil: learn to do well; seek judgement, relieve the oppressed, judge the fatherless, plead for the widow' (Is. 1/16, 17). On that showing alone it might be thought that the clean-unclean distinction simply symbolizes a moral right and wrong distinction.

That there is a moral reference in all these cases is undeniable, but I must go on to emphasize that something more was also involved. Whoredom, adultery, and murder, not only rendered those who committed them unclean in the sense of morally reprehensible, but also rendered them *unholy*. To assume that unholy simply means 'morally reprehensible' in these contexts is to beg the question. I would maintain that it means more. Physical health and cleanliness certainly symbolize moral goodness, but I would contend that both these symbolize something still further. In the Evening Prayer of confession included in the Book of Common Prayer we have the words: 'and there is no health in us' and this is not a reference to physical ill-health, nor even to offence against moral laws alone, but to offence 'against *thy holy* laws'.

Consider the case of leprosy for instance. From one point of view this disease is a purely physical matter, a case for medical inspection and attention. It was obviously this to the Hebrew as well, and he took what precaution he thought fit for preventing the spread of the disease, but the important thing for us is that the Hebrew thought of this situation as involving not only what we might call physical or even moral factors but something still more as well. We find, in Lev. Ch. 14, that if a leper was healed, a sacrifice of *atonement* was necessary (see especially Lev. 14/19, 20), and such an atonement is only mentioned in connection with *sin* and guilt. To the Hebrew the body-situation was also a soul-situation; a leper-situation was a sin-situation. To take another example, the author of I Peter describes Christ as a 'lamb without blemish and without spot' (I Peter 1/19). There is here a reference to Christ's character and person, and he is described in the same Epistle as the one 'who did *no sin*, neither was guile found in his mouth' (I Peter 2/22). He was not only free of all moral weakness but was also *sinless*. I will take yet another example from the New Testament. Upon passing a blind man the question that came naturally to the minds of Jesus' disciples was 'Who did sin, this man or his parents, that he should be born blind?' (John 9/2). Jesus himself did not share their rather naive view of the relation between sin and disease, still even he thought of the physical defect as pointing beyond to a wider breadth of the total situation. The blind man was to be cured, 'that the works of God should be made manifest in him' (John 9/3). It may not be particularly clear what this meant, but it certainly implies that the cure of the man born blind was symbolic of something greater than itself, yet of which it was a part. It is to be emphasized that these events and situations function symbolically just because they were themselves a part of what they symbolized. The healing of the leper was itself a part of the regaining of holiness, and so also was the cure of the blind man itself a part of what Christians call 'the coming of God's kingdom'.

So now we see that the holy situation could involve such

features as physical cleanness, physical health, moral clean-ness and health, and also something *more* than all this. It is this something *more* that makes the situation a *holy* one, but having said this I can go on to emphasize here the same point as I made above with regard to physical cleanness and health. The point is that though moral goodness does not itself constitute holiness, yet it is significant that it is the sort of thing that can harmonize with, and be incorporated in, that divine 'whole-ness' which is holiness. Moral evil can never take this position. Thus whatever the divine 'wholeness' is, it is evidently some-thing which, to use personal terms, 'prefers', 'chooses', moral goodness for special incorporation into itself rather than moral evil. This does not tell us everything we would like to know about 'divine wholeness' by a long way, but it is a step forward in the right direction. We have at least some hint of what the logical behaviour of the term 'divine whole' should be like.

The view that I have put forward in this chapter ties up with some of the points made in the preceding discussion of holiness as 'power'. There we saw that holiness is often thought of as a 'power' of life, but that it was never a 'power' that could be exhaustively accounted for in terms of the observable characteristics and physical changes of a living organism. Similarly, I have argued above that holiness means more than good physical health; holiness is a 'wholeness' that is more than mere physical wholeness. There is also a parallel in the further development of the discussion of power of life on the one hand, and health on the other. From a discussion of the power of living we were led to consider the power of living 'in its *deepest* and most *comprehensive* sense', that is, to the power of doing good not only in a moral sense but also in a special religious sense. So here again, a discussion of health led eventu-ally to a consideration of 'health' in its symbolic sense where it means moral goodness and, in the religious context, even more than this too.

Holiness is *more* than healthy living in both the physical and moral sense. But healthy living in both these senses is specially capable of harmonizing with this '*more*', whatever it may be. Since healthy living in both a physical and moral sense is especially the function of a person, then the implication seems to be that we should think of this 'more' too in personal terms. If we want to know why healthy and morally good living is in special harmony with the holy, and if we want suggestions as to what sort of harmony this is, then we shall have to consider more fully the question of divine personality.

I have so far deliberately avoided entering into any discussion of the separation which often seems to be implied in 'holiness'. This is an important matter which I must proceed to investigate in the next chapter.

CHAPTER VII

SEPARATEDNESS

THERE can be no doubt that holiness has always implied a separatedness of some kind or other. Not only is separatedness implied in the Greek word ἅγιος but there is the same implication in the Hebrew term קֹדֶשׁ too. Professor Norman Snaith points out that Baudissin, who wrote authoritatively on the Old Testament conception of holiness, held that 'the root' of קֹדֶשׁ (qodesh) 'originally meant "separation" in as much as it is clear that it deals with the things that belong to the gods as distinct from men'.[1] Helmer Ringgren, however, after making a comparative study of the root קדשׁ in the book to which I have already referred, comes to the conclusion that 'the idea of withdrawal, or separation, is not always very prominent.'[2] It seems to me that we may safely say that holiness has generally *implied* separatedness, but that it is rarely to be understood as being equivalent in meaning to 'separatedness'. Things, places and people have been regarded as 'separate' *because* they were holy, but the converse was not true. Nothing became holy merely by being separated from the sphere of ordinary things. It was only in virtue of its relation to God as his property that anything became holy, but since this did apparently imply being separated from something else we must find out what sort of separatedness is implied in holiness.

First of all I want to consider how special people, places and things are separated from ordinary people, places and things as being holy, and in the same context I must ask how this is compatible with the claim that everything, in some sense, belongs to God and is therefore holy. Secondly, it seems that the separatedness which seems to be implied in holiness is closely related with a certain tension in the experience of religious believers. This matter must also be discussed, and it will be seen

---

[1] *Distinctive Ideas of the Old Testament* p. 29-30. (Epworth Press, 1944).
[2] *The Prophetical Conception of Holiness* p. 6.

that this tension is further related to the development of eschatological views. Finally, I shall attempt to show how the separatedness in question may be helpfully understood in terms of separation between us and an ideal person.

THE SEPARATEDNESS OF SPECIAL PEOPLE, PLACES AND THINGS

Judging by some instances separatedness might appear to be a purely spatio-temporal matter of being on one side of a boundary-line rather than another. This is what the command given to Moses in Ex. 19/12 might on the face of it be taken to imply.[3] To take another example, the man from God in Ezekiel's vision speaks of a wall which makes 'separation between that which was holy and that which was common' (Ez. 42/20). All descriptions of Hebrew temples specify a 'holy place' which is separate from the outer courts. It was not that these areas were thought of as becoming holy through the act of setting them apart; rather, they were set apart because they were considered holy. Holiness, however, implied a separatedness that was more than spatio-temporal. The example of the holy mount in Ez. 42/20, for instance, should be considered in the light of what was said in my last chapter. There it was shown that the mount is considered holy because it belonged to God; it was his special property and dwelling place, and this implied that the mount was an extension of his personality. If this was so, the important thing was not so much the partition between two pieces of ground as the partition between what belonged to the 'wholeness' of Yahweh and what did not belong to him in quite the same way. We must not, of course, forget that the Hebrew also believed that the whole earth and the 'fulness thereof' was 'the Lord's'; 'the world, and they that dwell therein' (Ps. 24/1) belonged to him. Yet the Lord also had his special abode, his 'hill' which was 'his holy place', and though the Psalmist has just said that all that dwell in the earth belong to God, he still goes on to ask: 'Who shall ascend into the hill of the Lord? And who shall stand in his holy place?' (Ps. 24/3). Thus it seems that though everything belonged to God, the hill

[3] See last chapter (Holiness or Wholeness) p. 91.

was in a *special* sense his property, and that Yahweh was 'present' there in a special way. Similarly, Yahweh was thought to be *especially* 'present' in the holy of holies and in the holy ark. So also with regard to persons; though everybody is 'the Lord's', yet some people belong to him in a special sense and are in special close relationship with him. The Levites, the priests, the pure in heart and the righteous, were the ones who were qualified for this special privilege. It was not simply that these people became holy solely in virtue of their special function, or of their moral purity. Those factors came into it, but there was more as well. They belonged in a special sense to something beyond themselves, that is, to what I have called a 'divine personal wholeness', and to exist in this special relation also implied being separate from what was ordinary or profane.[4]

It might be thought that, since everything was thought of as belonging in some sense to God, everything and everybody would be holy, and there are indeed instances in the Old Testament where the word 'holy' is applied not only to a special particular space in the temple but to the whole of the country in which the Israelites lived; it is called the 'holy land' (Zech. 2/12). Again, there are instances where holiness is attributed not only to the priests and Levites but to the whole people of Israel: 'for thou art an holy people unto the Lord thy God' (Deut. 7/6). Thus it would appear that even the ordinary sphere of life could also be considered in some sense holy. Yet, was not the wall of the temple intended 'to make a separation between that which was holy and that which was common?' (Ez. 42/20). This seems to imply that the land outside the temple was not holy. Clearly there must have been a difference between the holiness of special places and special people, such as the holy of holies and the priests on the one hand, and on the other, the holiness of the holy land and of the holy people of Israel.

One way out of this difficulty would be to think of the special holy things, places and people as symbolizing or representing the whole area and the whole people of Israel. It has been maintained that 'together with the priest and the prophet

---

[4] 'Profane' usually translates הלל which means 'open to common use'.

the king was one of the "upholders of holiness" '.[5] This holiness, I take it, would be that of the whole tribe. This is in accord with the fact, mentioned by Ringgren, that 'cult is the normal way of getting into contact with the divinity'.[6] If this view were accepted then the holiness of special places and special people would not be due to any peculiar property belonging to them as distinct from everything and everyone else, but rather to their special function in connection with the 'wholeness' which extended beyond themselves. It was a 'wholeness' which extended beyond them into the general life of the Israelites on the one hand, and which had Yahweh as its divine personal centre on the other. On this interpretation, the separatedness between special holy things and places was not of importance in *itself*, but was representative of the separation between the 'divine whole' which could include the whole of Hebrew life and that which did not belong to that 'whole'. Thus, when the priest was consecrated, and when he washed himself and his garments, or when he put on special garments before performing the holy rites, it was not these observable performances in themselves that were important, but something more which they symbolized. This explanation could be extended to all cases of things, places and persons which are 'set apart' as being holy. It is not the mere observable aspect of the 'setting apart', whatever form it may take, that is important but the 'more' which belongs to the wider breadth of the total situation.

It seems to me that Paul Tillich has something very much like this in view when he discusses the same problem in his book *The Protestant Era*. His discussion of nature and sacrament leads him to a point where it might be inferred 'that the Protestant interpretation of nature would attribute sacramental qualities to everything'.[7] He has to admit that it is not quite so. 'The holy,' he says, 'appears only in special places, in special contexts.'[7] There is, however, a danger that 'the "special places", the peculiar materials, the ritual performances, which are connected with a sacrament claim holiness for themselves'.[7] That is, Tillich thinks it is a mistake to fasten our attention exclu-

[5] *The Old Testament and Modern Study* p. 295. (Ed. H. H. Rowley, Oxford, 1952).
[6] *The Prophetical Conception of Holiness* p. 8.
[7] *The Protestant Era* p. 123.

sively on to the spatio-temporal characteristics of the holy situation, for holiness is something more which can stand in relation to any observable phenomena. The holiness of special places, rites and so forth, 'is a representation of what essentially is possible in everything and every place'.[8] He holds that the 'bread of the sacrament stands for all bread and ultimately for all nature'.[9] This does not mean to say that holiness is simply nature as a totality of observable phenomena. He tells us later that 'nature must be brought into the unity of the history of salvation'.[10] It would take us too far off the course of my thesis to consider what Tillich means by 'the history of salvation'; it is sufficient to note that the unity involved here is more than a mere spatio-temporal unity. I have referred to it as a 'divine personal whole'; Tillich would prefer such a term as the 'Unconditioned' or 'the ground of all being'.

Two points from the interpretation I have just given require to be taken up. In the first place, it seems that the Hebrews thought that the holy was definitely separated from something or other. I have suggested that the real separation was not so much between the ordinary sphere of life and the special holy places, things and people specified in their cultic rules, but between the 'divine whole', to which Israel as a nation could belong, and anything that does not belong to this 'divine whole'. The question arises: what is it that is separate from the 'divine whole'? The Hebrew thought that there were certain things which most definitely lie outside the divine sphere. For instance, unclean things such as carcasses, or unclean people such as the leper, were kept separate on the ground that they were a real threat to one's relation to the holy. It seems that there was a definite boundary in relation to which one had to be on the one side or the other, that is, one had to refrain from contact with the unclean or else suffer a break away from the 'divine whole'. As with unclean things, so also with immoral practices and immoral people. They had to be kept separate or else holiness would be lost.

What I have said in the previous chapter should be brought to bear on this point too. There, I showed how uncleanness

<hr>

[8] *The Protestant Era* p 124.   [9] *ibid.* p. 124.
[10] ibid. p. 125.

involved 'more' for the Hebrew than just physical disease or abnormality. Not only did I emphasize how moral elements came into the situation as well (in the case of the leper for instance), but I tried to show that something further was involved. Holiness implied separation not only from physical and moral disease but from *sin*. I shall have to go deeper into the significance of religious good and evil as being something more than mere moral right and wrong in the next chapter. What I want to emphasize just now is that something *more* than the observable characteristics of disease is involved here and something *more* too than the observable characteristics of wrong action. This 'more' is indicated by the use of the word 'sin' in these contexts. A. G. Hebert, expounding the Old Testament view of sin says that 'the essence of Sin lies in a wrong relation to the personal God'.[11] And it seems to me that, whatever the external manifestations of sin may be, there is *more* than that in the situation; there is something which is expressible in such terms as 'breach in the relations which should exist between man and God',[12] or 'alienation from God'.[13] This leads us to a tautology, for I began by asking what is it that is separate from the 'divine whole', and now it seems that the answer is that it is just that which is separate from the 'divine whole'. Separation from God is separation from God. Such a tautology is not without its significance however, for it is yet another way of emphasizing how extraordinary is that separatedness which is involved in holiness. If we are to know what separation from the 'divine personal whole' involves then we have to know what the 'divine personal whole' means.

TENSION

I now come to the second point which arises out of my interpretation of 'separation', and out of what Tillich said in the account which I mentioned as being similar to the one I offered. Tillich held that special holy places, things and so forth, represent what 'essentially is possible' everywhere and in everything. It is possible that the whole of nature should be, to use

[11] *The Bible from Within* p. 29. (Oxford, 1952).
[12] *The Old Testament and Modern Study* p. 354.
[13] J. S. Whale, *Christian Doctrine*. (Cambridge, 1950) p. 45.

my own terminology, in a harmonious union with the 'divine personal whole', but is it in fact so? It might be expected that the answer here should be a simple 'yes' or 'no', but such an answer cannot be given. Rather, it appears that religious people have at all times felt themselves to be in a state of tension between having a right relation to the holy and being alienated from the holy.

This tension is certainly in evidence in the life of the Hebrew believer, sometimes it seems that the Hebrew felt himself to be in a right relationship with the 'wholeness' which made him holy; sometimes it would appear that the opposite was true. We have seen how Israel is sometimes called holy—a holy land and a holy people—and this would seem to imply that they actually were in a proper relation with their God and that they were indeed within the sphere of his 'wholeness'. But we also read that the Hebrews fell into the sin of turning their backs on Yahweh: 'they have despised the Holy One of Israel, they are estranged and gone backward' (Is. 1/4). The very necessity for the injunction: 'sanctify yourselves therefore, and be ye holy; for I am holy' (Lev. 11/44) suggests that there was a tendency to fall away from this standard. In a sense Israel was a holy nation; in a sense it was not. So far as it upheld and observed the cult it was holy; so far as it failed to do so, it was not. At the one extreme there was the influence of the priests who could approach the holy of holies, and at the other there was the influence of the miserable offenders who became unclean, and spread uncleanness through their moral abuses. The former was constantly giving cause for calm and confidence, while the latter was a constant source of fear and dread.

The position of the ordinary Israelite therefore involved a tension between the desire to be on the right side of the holy/ unholy line of separation, and an inherent tendency to fall on the wrong side. This striving for holiness against the current of tendencies towards that which is incompatible with it is characteristic of all the Old Testament Hebrew religion, as well as of the early Christian Church and the whole of Christianity subsequent to this. The choice for humanity would seem to be a clear and simple one between (a) being separate from the holy, and (b) being united with the holy and separated from that which is incompatible with the holy. Yet the picture is not quite as clear and simple as that, for there is this half-way position which the great majority of Hebrews occupied and which the great majority of Christians have always occupied. Within this middle position there is room for a gradation from the less, to the more, holy.

This tension was not simply a matter of subjective experience, but was felt to be in evidence in the creation as well. Sometimes it was felt that the world was in harmony with the 'divine whole' but at other times it was felt that disunity and chaos prevailed. As Ludwig Köhler says 'the world of men is continually threatened and assailed by the destructive powers of chaos'.[14] Creation constituted a victory for the power of life over the powers of chaos, and the following of winter by summer signified the victory of the power of life over death.[15] The Hebrew would interpret the deliverance from Egypt in a similar light. Whenever he thought of creation, the renewal of life before the harvest season, and the deliverance from Egypt, then he would have reason to be calm and confident, for the universe was kindly towards him and favoured conditions of life and thrift. Adversities, trials and death brought fear and dread. The former situation implied a right relation with the holy. A friendly world meant a holy situation, an unfriendly world implied an unholy one.

Holiness was the very foundation of the Hebrew's existence; to be or not to be on proper terms with the holy was a matter of life and death. Köhler, describing Hebrew thought, says: 'if God were not there, chaos might become master of the earth, and disaster be upon us. Thus, deep in his consciousness there slumbers a continual insecurity, and one which sometimes becomes wakeful and alive.'[16] The horrors of flood and famine would naturally arouse these anxieties which made the Hebrew ask with urgency 'Will the sun rise? Will the rains come? Will harvest follow on seed-time?'[17] And, to quote Köhler again, 'in a whole host of myths and stories we can still detect that tremendous tension, so important for life, which is expressed in these and similar questions'.[17]

[14] *The Hebrew Man* p. 128. (S.C.M. Press, 1956).   [15] *See ibid.* pp. 127-9.
[16] *ibid.* p. 128.   [17] *ibid.* p. 129.

The cause of the Hebrew's insecurity and experience of
tension would be, partly at any rate, the fact that these vital
factors seemed beyond his direct control, but there was for him
however one source of solace and comfort, namely, the cult of
his religion. Here there was some hope of his making a contribution which would make a difference to the situation. The
Hebrew believed that by observing the cult he could, to some
degree, decide whether the world would be a friendly or unfriendly one. 'In the cult man comes into contact with the
divine power through which alone the factors which make for
his weal or woe may be controlled.'[18]

This brings us back to a point which I have already stressed,
namely, that the Hebrews thought of the power which controlled their environment as being personal. They thought of
their whole life, their necessities, their environment, as somehow depending upon a being who was in some respects similar
to human beings, a being who could support life or bring
destruction as he wished. The Hebrews often behaved as though
the holy power was a person, anthropomorphically conceived
—a person who could be appeased by gifts or indignantly
aroused by offensive behaviour, a person who hoped, was dis-
appointed, and could repent of having begun a particular project, a very powerful person who could express his good will,
wrath, disappointments by pulling the strings which controlled
the basic necessities of human life on earth. The cult can now
be seen as an attempt to get into contact with this being, to get
on good terms with him, for he could be appeased or alienated.

A crude anthropomorphic view of God is open to many
serious objections, but we should not assume that the Hebrew
took his own anthropomorphical terminology literally. On the
contrary, there are indications that he thought of the controller
of his environment as being a very exceptional kind of person,
a person who was beyond comprehension by the imagination
of man. Yahweh was such that the prophet asked: 'To whom
then will ye liken God? or what likeness will ye compare unto
him?' (Is. 40/18). To come into harmony with such a being
would not be a matter of pulling levers in a mechanical set-up,
or of bribing an earthly monarch, but something far greater.

[18] *The Old Testament and Modern Study* p. 292.

Similarly, separation from the 'divine whole' could not be completely understood in terms of disease, famine and enemy destruction. The observable events were symptomatic of a deeper cleft. Again, the observation of cultic demands was not always a simple matter, especially since they involved moral precepts, and the Hebrew would often fail to live up to the law. But again, alienation from Yahweh meant something more than this too. If being in harmony with, or separate from, the 'holy one' were merely an observable matter of succeeding, or failing, to comply with cultic precepts, and of enjoying, or being deprived of, certain tangible benefits, then the Hebrew could have been fairly certain as to where he stood in his relation to Yahweh. The very ambiguity of his position, and the tension he experienced, suggest that being with, or separated from, the 'holy one' was something that could not be precisely tracked down in observational language.

Eventually, the Hebrew gave expression to the ambiguity of his predicament in eschatological terms. It is a matter of debate whether eschatology developed early or late in Hebrew religion, but we must agree that at some point or other 'present experience of the divine power, renewed annually in the festival, had been transformed into future hope'.[19] Speaking of the Hebrew view of the social order, G. Ernest Wright says that 'the *revealed* order and the *actual* order are never identical except in the eschatological age to which history is moving by the direction and intervention of God'.[20] Yet, there was a sense in which the Hebrews' situation was, there and then, holy, for it would be unbearable for a people who believed as they did if it were not so. The holy power was the power which was the very source of life itself. So how could it be possible to live, especially to live well, to live righteously, without the presence of the holy power?

The points that I have made above hold in the case of Christianity as well as in early Hebrew religion. This can be shown by a reference to the Christian views of baptism for instance. Of all Christian rituals, baptism has the strongest claim to be considered as a transition point from the unholy to the holy

[19] *The Old Testament and Modern Study* p. 304.
[20] *The Old Testament Against its Environment* p. 45. (S.C.M. Press, 1950).

sphere. It is, like circumcision amongst the Hebrews, a mark of separation. This point is clearly made in Dr Dillistone's *Christianity and Symbolism* where he says that 'so long as there continued to be a steady flow of converts from paganism into the Church, the notes of separation and renunciation never ceased to be sounded in the baptismal ceremony'.[21]

Various aspects of the rite of baptism have been emphasized by various Christian theologians, and one aspect that is as prominent as any is that which views baptism as 'marking a radical break, a renunciation, a reversal, a repudiation of the world, the flesh and the devil, a death to sin and a new life of righteousness—in fact which sees it as marking a moral crisis of quite unique importance'.[22] We find packed in this quotation a reference to all the aspects of the Old Testament holy/unholy separatedness. There is the line of demarcation indicated by the words 'break', 'renunciation', 'reversal', 'repudiation'; there are the two sides of this line, one of which is the sphere of the flesh, the devil, and sin, while the other is the sphere of 'new life', which is moreover life of 'righteousness'; and there is also a 'crossing over' indicated in the reference to 'death' and 'moral crisis'. Also, most important of all, there is an indication that though the critical situation involves moral factors it is more than just a matter of abandoning an immoral life for a moral one. *This* moral crisis is one of 'unique importance'; it is a '*death*' which initiates a new 'life'. The extraordinary aspect of the situation receives a new emphasis when it is further argued that 'baptism is above all, a symbol of the Death and Resurrection of Christ and so of the believer',[23] or, to quote St Paul for the same view, 'know ye not, that so many of us as were baptized into Jesus Christ were baptized into His death that like as Christ was raised up from the dead . . . even so we also should walk in newness of life' (Rom. 6/3-4).[24] These last words, no doubt, have a moral connotation, but it is equally obvious that something much more than this is meant. The words 'death', 'unique moral crisis' and 'newness of life' are

---

[21] *Christianity and Symbolism* p. 214. (Collins, 1955).
[22] ibid. p. 212.
[23] ibid. p. 215 .
[24] *Authorized Version.*

here used to refer to a 'cross-over' or 'change-over' from a state of alienation and separation from the 'divine personal whole', to a state of harmony with, and participation in, that 'whole'.

The picture just given might lead us to think that there is a clear and distinct demarcation line between the holy and the unholy and that to cross over from the one side to the other is a definite, irrevocable step which would not leave much room for the middle, ambiguous area of striving and tension which has hitherto figured in my discussion of separatedness. Such a picture should not, however, be taken too literally for in Christianity, as in Hebrew religion, the position of the religious believer is not easy to define. In a sense he enters into a right relation with the holy at baptism, yet there is a sense in which right relationship with the holy is something still to be achieved in the future. Luther, who emphasized so much (as did St Paul himself too) the clear life and death character of the baptismal 'cross-over', has to admit that, so far as actual circumstances are concerned, things are not so clearly defined. He is quoted as saying: 'thus thou hast been baptized once for all sacramentally but thou needest continually to be baptized by faith, and must continually die and continually live'.[25] In Christianity, as in Old Testament Hebrew religion, the holy situation seems sometimes to be present, sometimes not. Sometimes it would seem that the Church, the New Israel, the body of Christ are a holy people, yet in a sense they are only on the way to being holy. Bethune-Baker points out that 'though St Paul addressed the first generation of Christians as "saints" or "holy", it is clear from his letters to them that they were so potentially only, and that he applied the term to them as set apart (called out from the rest of men) for a holy purpose, rather than possessed of personal holiness'.[26] The Christian idea often is that the true holy situation in which men can find themselves must belong to some future date, but that the holiness of that future situation is in some sense appropriated by the church even now. This point is well expressed by Dr Dillistone when he says that 'the baptism of the individual believer is to be regarded as the

[25] *Christianity and Symbolism* p. 215.
[26] *The Early History of Christian Doctrine* p. 357.

proleptic realization of his final deliverance from sin and his establishment in righteousness in the Kingdom of God'.[27] This must surely be Dr Thornton's point too, when he holds that 'in baptism the neophyte becomes partaker in that final "regeneration when the Son of man shall sit on the throne of his glory". . . . In every baptism therefore *starting point and goal are one.* The Last Day *began to dawn* for each of us on the first day of our life in Christ.'[28] The tension of which I have spoken is possibly nowhere better stressed than in the Westminster Confession's exposition of baptism. There the baptism is described as a seal of our ingrafting into Christ which implies a partaking of the benefits of the covenant of grace, but everything is not completed in the baptismal rite itself for the people are enjoined 'to improve and make the right use of their Baptism; and of the Covenant sealed thereby betwixt God and their souls'.[29] We are, in baptism, by the Covenant of God made inheritors of holiness, but it is up to us to make use of, or to repudiate, the inheritance. Grace for holiness is a promise of the being whom Christians call 'God', and the baptized person stands in a position where he can go forward and realize the promise, or go back and ignore it. This is the 'moral crisis of quite unique importance' of which Dr Dillistone spoke.

Two points have been brought to the fore in the present chapter. Firstly, it has been shown that to be united with, or separated from, the holy is not purely a matter of performing or not performing the outward ceremonies which were involved in the cultus, or of going through the ceremony of baptism as a mere observable event. To be united with, or separate from the holy is not a matter of conforming, or failing to conform, with certain moral precepts either. It is something more than all this, and I have described it as a matter of being in a right or wrong relation with a 'divine personal whole'. Secondly, I have tried to show that this relation is not at all easy to define, and that a static picture of it is misleading. It is not that one is, or is not, at a certain moment in a right relation with the holy, but that one is, or is not, in the *process* of coming

[27] *Christianity and Symbolism* p. 217 (my italics).
[28] *The Common Life in the Body of Christ* p. 191 (my italics). (A & C. Black, 1950).
[29] *Directory of Public Worship A.D. 1644.*

into the right relation. The best that one could say is that something has already been achieved, yet much more is to be fulfilled. But we need a better philosophical understanding of what this means, and it would help us in this respect if we could find a suitable model which would lend itself to qualification in such a way as to function somewhat like the term 'divine personal whole'. What I mean by such a qualified model should become clear as I discuss some candidates which seem suitable.

IDEALS AND THE IDEAL PERSON

Let us consider first what I shall call a limited ideal. Not all ideals are limited, but the ones that are can in principle be clearly defined. When in certain cases we describe certain conditions as 'ideal', we are quite clear as to what the ideal consists in. For instance, the 'ideals' in 'Ideal Homes' exhibitions are plainly observable; they are the sort of things that can be described in observational terms. We can also imagine what it would be to aspire after such an ideal home of our own and, with modern furniture plans, it is possible to do this by degrees. At any stage short of complete fulfilment of ideal one could say that it was partly achieved but not completely fulfilled—the ideal is then in *process* of being achieved.

Now let us consider another model which has all the features of this first one but also far more, a model which suggests the sort of situation in which religious believers find themselves. We can use the word 'home' in a different sense to mean, not observable furniture and fittings this time, but the sphere of family life. We might describe our ideal in this case as a 'happy home', but this time it is not a limited, clearly definable ideal. Happiness is more than a sum of observable actions as John Wisdom showed with the help of a quotation from J. P. Marquand's novel *H.M. Pulham, Esq.* In his attempt to explain what happiness is Pulham says: All the things that two people do together, two people like Kay and me, add up to something. There are the kids and the house and the dog and all the people we have known and all the times we've been out to dinner. Of course, Kay and I do quarrel sometimes but when you add it all together, all of it isn't as bad as the parts of it seem.'[30] Many people would claim that their's was a happy home, yet if asked whether or not it was *ideal* we should probably hesitate. We should not like to say that there was nothing of the ideal in it, on the contrary, we might even describe it as the 'best of homes'. Yet, the very word 'ideal' presents a challenge which makes us hesitate. After all, we do not claim perfection for ourselves as individuals or for the other members of our family. So how could the home be ideal? In one popular sense it may have been 'ideal', but we can always imagine the possibility of there being a still higher standard which suggests that we should not use the word 'ideal' of anything we have yet experienced. What I have just said is true of other ideals too, such as the ideal of moral behaviour for example.

What I would suggest is that the 'whole' which is holiness could be thought of as an ideal. This time, however, it would not be a particular ideal relating to a particular field of life. The word 'ideal' should now be qualified by such a term as 'perfect' or 'absolute'. Such an 'ideal' would incorporate all others, but it would also surpass them as well. For instance, it would include ideal homes in the sense of material welfare, and homes which were ideal in happiness, but it would also imply far more. In so far as furniture and the external behaviour of the members of a family came into it, it would have an empirical reference, but it would of course be far more than anything describable in observational terms. It was thus, I would suggest, that the Hebrew thought of the holy. It implied material success, but something more as well; it implied a good moral life, but something more than that even. Material success, good health, and moral righteousness were specially apt to harmonize with the 'wholeness' which is holiness, but the 'wholeness' itself was more than all this. Similarly, we could hold that good conditions of living, good health and moral uprighteousness are specially apt to harmonize with the 'absolute ideal', but this 'ideal' itself is more than the sum of these conditions. In so far as such conditions prevail we have reason to believe that the world is in harmony with the 'ideal' but in so far as these conditions are lacking we have reason to fear that

[30] *Logic and Language.* (First Series) p. 191.

the 'ideal' still belongs to a future more or less remote. The ideal must be separate from the ordinary in so far as the ordinary does not reach the standard of the 'ideal', yet the ideal may be partly realized in ordinary life.

Now I come to a different model. I am thinking here of our relationship to a person when we get to know him. We can, in the first place, get to know a person as a body with certain characteristics. Part of what we mean by knowing a person is being able to recognize him by the colour of his hair, the shape of his head and so forth. At this level we could know a person more or less completely in a comparatively short time, and then there would be nothing more to learn. But to know a person properly means more than this; it involves knowing his character, his way of thinking, his point of view, his temperament and his disposition. Knowledge of a person in this sense is acquired only by degrees, and it is rarely, if ever, that we get to know a person perfectly. In so far as we do know him then we can communicate with him, associate with him, co-operate with him and so forth, but in so far as there is an aspect of his person that we do not know then, to that extent, we are separate, 'cut off', from him.

There is here again a parallel with the case of our relation to the 'divine whole', or our relation to the 'absolute ideal'. Let us now introduce a qualifier here too, and call the person in question 'perfect'. Here I am envisaging the possibility of there being a person such that however far we went in our knowledge of him he was still beyond us, still *more* than what we already know of him. Such a person would be separate from us, yet in so far as we know him at all we should enjoy positive relationship with him. We sometimes estimate a man's personality by noting his physical features. Sometimes we succeed to a small extent; more often we fail, though there may be a possibility of improvement in this exercise. People have claimed that they 'see' God in the universe considered as physical phenomena and in certain physical events; but just as often men have been baffled by the evidence. As the ordinary person is more than what his physical features suggest, so the 'perfect person' is more than what the observable universe suggests.

These two qualified models do not provide us with straight-

122

forward simple answers to the questions: what is holiness? and, what sort of separatedness is implied in it? I have done little more than suggest alternative logical routes by following which we may hope to arrive at a better understanding of those questions. We must now travel further along these logical routes. Therefore, in the following chapter I shall examine more thoroughly the connection between morals and holiness. Following that, I must come to grips with the question of divine personality.

CHAPTER VIII

HOLINESS AND MORAL GOODNESS

THE NUMINOUS

I SHALL begin this examination of the relation between holiness and morals with a reference to the views of Rudolf Otto who distinguishes holiness from moral values, and selects the former for special attention and analysis. Otto asserts that ' "Holiness" —"the holy"—is a category of interpretation and valuation peculiar to the sphere of religion';[1] it is a 'quite distinctive category'.[2] The common practice of taking the word 'holy' as meaning 'completely good' is rejected. Otto claims that this usage is inaccurate in that, though 'this moral significance is contained in the word',[3] it neglects something that the word 'includes in addition, . . . a clear overplus of meaning',[3] which he wishes to isolate. Of the term οἰάγιοι,* he says, 'it is manifest at once that this does not mean "the morally perfect" people'.[4]

It is true that there has often been a tendency amongst religious thinkers to speak in the way which Otto criticizes. When Harnack says of the Lutheran Church that 'it neglected far too much the moral problem, the "Be ye holy, for I am holy" ',[5] it does indeed look as though he thought of holiness as being morality and nothing more. This tendency to equate holiness with morality may have received a great impetus through a certain interpretation of the views of Kant. As F. E. England

---

[1] *The Idea of the Holy* p. 5.   [2] ibid. p. 4.
[3] ibid. p. 5.
* It is worth noting that ὅσιος which is also translated 'holy' is nearly always found in an ethical setting where it seems to mean 'pious' and 'just'. See, for example, Tit. 1/8 where the word is surrounded by such epithets as 'given to hospitality', 'a lover of good', 'sober-minded', 'just' and 'temperate'. However, even ὅσιος sometimes implies something more than moral goodness. In Heb. 7/26 Christ himself is described as ὅσιος and there it is added not only that he was guileless and undefiled, but also that he was 'separated from *sinners*' (my italics). See my remarks about sin on p. 131f.
[4] ibid. p. 86.
[5] *History of Dogma* Vol. III p. 267. (Williams & Norgate, 1899).

has pointed out, in Kant's philosophy 'God himself is declared to be holy on the ground of the coincidence of his will with the pure moral law'.[6] This could be taken in either of two ways. One might take it to mean that our ordinary moral principles are the measure of God's will and so the ground of his holiness. Or one might take it as implying that the moral law itself is in this case something exceptional, and more than just an ordinary moral principle. If the former interpretation were followed, it would lead to the tendency which Otto deplores. In any case, the tendency was very real in the last century as Elliott-Binns makes clear in his book *English Thought—The Theological Aspect.* He writes, 'when *Ecce Homo* was published in 1866 Westcott commented: "It is this so-called Christian morality as the 'sum of the Gospel' which makes Christianity so powerless now." '[7] The implication here is of course that the 'sum of the Gospel' is really much *more* than ordinary morality and *more* than this *so-called* Christian morality too. In so far as there was this tendency to regard 'the sum of the Gospel' as mere morality then we can sympathize with Otto's discontent.

Otto is not satisfied with saying that 'holy' means more than 'moral' but goes on to maintain that the 'overplus' or 'extra' which he calls the 'numinous' is the original meaning of 'holy', and especially of the word in its Latin, Greek and Semitic forms. This view is well supported by Old Testament scholars. Ringgren tells us that 'it is remarkable that the ethical aspect of holiness plays a very subordinate part in prophetic preaching',[8] and Mowinckel, in the latest of his works to appear in English—*He That Cometh*—says that 'the word "holy" practically never has any ethical reference in the Old Testament'.[9] This is also Fison's view in *The Blessing of the Holy Spirit* where he holds that 'to begin with, the moral connotation is no necessary part of the Hebrew idea of the holy at all . . .'.[10]

Otto devotes the greater part of his book to an analysis of the 'unique original feeling-response, which can be in itself

---

[6] *Kant's Conception of God* p. 179. (Allen & Unwin, 1929).
[7] *English Thought—The Theological Aspect* p. 228-9. (Longmans, 1956).
[8] *The Prophetical Conception of Holiness* p. 23.
[9] *He That Cometh* p. 381n. (Blackwell, 1956).
[10] *The Blessing of the Holy Spirit* p. 50. (Longmans, Green, 1950).

ethically neutral and claims consideration in its own rights'.[11] He also speaks of a 'numinous' state of mind which is 'perfectly *sui generis* and irreducible to any other',[12] a state which can be discussed but not strictly defined. It is important to bear in mind that the 'feeling-response' or 'numinous state of mind' has an object corresponding to it, an object which is called 'the numinous'.[13] 'There must be felt a something "numinous", something bearing the character of a "numen", to which the mind turns spontaneously.'[13] Otto explicitly tells us that 'the numinous is thus felt as objective and outside the self'.[13] Though this object cannot be described or defined, man can pass upon it a 'judgement of *appreciation* of a unique kind'.[14] It is a value, 'objective and ultimate',[14] 'precious beyond all conceiving', and is in an 'absolute sense worthy to be praised'.[15]

Otto is fully aware of the undeniably close connection between holiness and morals, and he puts forward a theory to account for this connection. It is a theory of 'schematization', but this word does not give much of a clue as to what Otto has in mind. He refers to the psychological fact of the association of ideas, whereby an idea x, is closely associated with, and can therefore easily by mistakenly substituted for, an idea y. Thus there is the possibility of x arousing in us the feeling appropriate to y. The numinous feeling, though actually *sui generis*, has numerous associations with others, 'and therefore it and they may reciprocally excite or stimulate one another and cause one another to appear in the mind'.[16] In passing, one should note that Otto often speaks of a numinous 'feeling' and a numinous 'state of mind' as though they were the same thing, hence his account of association of ideas and subsequent cross-association of feelings is not as clear as it might be. However, he goes on to say that the association of ideas can, under certain circumstances, set up lasting combinations and connections, and this is held to be as true in the case of feeling as in the case of ideas. 'Accordingly, we see religious feeling in permanent connection with other feelings which are conjoined to it in accordance with this principle of Association.'[17]

[11] *The Idea of the Holy* p. 6.   [12] *ibid.* p. 7.
[13] *ibid.* p. 11.   [14] ibid. p. 53.
[15] ibid. p. 54.   [16] *ibid.* p. 45.
[17] ibid. p. 46.

It is when the casual connection has turned into a permanent one that schematization occurs. We can, he maintains, see that schematism is a genuine one, as contrasted with a mere combination of analogies, 'from the fact that it does not fall to pieces, and cannot be cut out as the development of the consciousness of religious truth proceeds onwards and upwards, but is only recognized with greater definiteness and certainty'.[18] So great is Otto's desire to stress the permanence of the connection here that he takes the rather uncomfortable step of saying that it is like the Kantian connection between a Category and its temporal schema. It is very difficult to see that the type of schematism which Otto describes with reference to the association of ideas is anything like the Kantian schematism. Kant's schemata are 'nothing but a priori determinations of time according to rules.'[19] Otto's schemata are the rational elements of religion of which an example is 'the sublime', while the category which is schematized is the non-rational, indescribable, undefinable 'holy'—whether it is the numinous feeling or the numinous object is not explained. The Kantian schemata and categories are quite different from Otto's. It may be that Otto only wants to emphasize that the *relation* between schemata and category is similar in both cases, but again this cannot possibly be so, for Otto's exposition in terms of associations of ideas is different altogether from the Kantian exposition of the relation of schemata to the categories. What is evident however is that Otto is very anxious to maintain a very close and essential connection between the rational and non-rational, the connection between the holy and, for instance, ethical goodness, while at the same time keeping a clear distinction between the two.

OTTO CRITICIZED

Otto's attempt to explain the relation of holiness with morality is not successful by a long way, and one must agree with John Oman that 'the attempt to relate the rational to the non-rational is the weakest part of the whole book'.[20] Otto only

---

[18] *The Idea of the Holy* p. 47.
[19] *Critique of Pure Reason* p. 121. (Dent Everyman Library, 1950).
[20] *Journal of Theological Studies Vol. XXV* p. 285.

succeeds in reiterating the fact that the holy is closely related to ethics and morality; he does not explain how they are related.[21]

Any full appraisal of Otto's work must contain a reference to John Oman's criticisms which appear in the latter's review of *The Idea of the Holy* in the *Journal of Theological Studies* Volume XXV, in his book *The Natural and the Supernatural* and in his contribution to *Science, Religion and Reality* under the title 'The Sphere of Religion'. Oman thinks that there is nothing distinctively religious in the non-rational numinous feeling which Otto presents as the fundamental element in religion. Such a feeling could not be differentiated from the spooky which even an animal might experience, and a religion which has this feeling as its basis can only be a superstition. Oman links Otto with Schleiermacher in a remark that is equally derogatory of both: 'Schleiermacher is in danger of ending in an artistic mystical feeling, and Professor Otto of a superstitious mystical awe; and which is worse?'[22] By contrast, Oman would have us remember that the sense of the holy is always related to an objective, environmental background, a background which is sacred and of absolute ethical value and worth. Otto's fault is to divorce 'the sense of the holy from any sense of an environment which is becoming for man an ethical reality'.[23] It is by reference to this environment that the feeling and sense of the holy can be distinguished from either primitive dread or modern artistic sense of the sublime.

Perhaps Oman's own position is not really quite so far removed from that of Otto as the former's criticisms suggest. After all, Otto is far from denying that the holy has any connection whatever with morality, as is obvious when he says, upon referring to the Hebrew *qādôsh*, the Greek ἅγιος, and the Latin *sanctus* and *sacer*, that 'it is not, of course, disputed, that these terms in all three languages connote, as part of their meaning, *good*, *absolute goodness*, when, that is, the notion has ripened and reached the highest stage in its development'.[24]

[21] Cf. F. E. England's criticism in Ch. 7 of his book *The Validity of Religious Experience*. (Nicholson & Watson, 1937).
[22] *Journal of Theological Studies* Vol. XXV p. 284.
[23] *Science, Religion and Reality* p. 287. (Sheldon Press, 1926).
[24] *The Idea of the Holy* p. 6.

What Otto is concerned to make clear is that though holiness does mean this, it also means more, and he explains that in his book he wants to draw special attention to this ' "extra" in the meaning of "holy" above and beyond the meaning of goodness'.[25] He claims that this, rather than the moral connotation, is the original and essential meaning of holiness. Oman counterclaims that in the evolution of the sense of the holy 'it is not difficult to discover, in every stage known to us, the germ at least of the moral developments',[26] but the quotations from modern scholars which appear at the beginning of this chapter suggest that Otto is nearer the mark on this point. Strangely enough Oman himself, after noting that 'in every Western European language, as well as our own, the term "holy" used by itself would be understood to mean what stirs moral reverence', goes on to say 'but this is not its original meaning', and adds 'the more religions are primitive, the more the holy has to do with awe, and less with moral reverence'.[27] On this showing Oman is not quite so distant from Otto as he sometimes makes himself out to be.

Oman may be right in suggesting that the non-rational feelings, which feature so prominently in Otto's book, are not sufficiently clearly distinguished from the spooky. At any rate, Otto does not make it clear enough *how* they could be distinguished, but it seems clear to me that he *does want* to distinguish them. The feeling is described as a kind of 'shuddering', but Otto emphasizes that he does not mean an ordinary shuddering: he thinks of it as being 'something more than "natural", ordinary fear'.[28] Again, 'it implies the first application of a category of valuation which has no place in the everyday natural world of ordinary experience, and is only possible to a being in whom has been awakened a mental predisposition, unique in kind, and different in a definite way from any "natural" faculty'.[29] This could hardly be the spooky: Otto has tried to show how very closely conjoined are the irrational feelings of the numinous and its rational schemata such as moral good-

[25] *The Idea of the Holy* p. 6 & 7.
[26] *The Natural and the Supernatural* p. 63. (Cambridge, 1931).
[27] *The Natural and the Supernatural* p. 59.
[28] *The Idea of the Holy* p. 15.
[29] ibid. p. 15·6.

ness. His attempt to do this was admittedly disappointing, but one thing is shown thereby, namely, that Otto did think of the numinous as being something different from the spooky. Oman is right in attacking Otto's schematism itself as a weakness in the argument, but we have to recognize at the same time that the mere attempt to schematize bears witness to the fact that the numinous was, for Otto, not so very different from what Oman calls 'the *direct sense* or *feeling* of the Supernatural'.[30]

Again, Oman gives the impression that Otto confines himself to a purely subjective emphasis on feeling, and ignores completely the sort of objective and evaluative reference which Oman himself would like to bring into the picture. In *The Natural and the Supernatural*, after pointing out that the sense of the holy as mere feeling is indistinguishable from the magical feeling of the spooky or the artistic sublime, he goes on to say that 'when we relate it to the absolute value of the sacred, we see at once that its awe has a quality different from dread, and its reverence from the sense even of the sublime'.[31] But Otto, too, has clearly maintained that the holy is such that he who experiences it passes upon it a 'judgement of *appreciation* of a unique kind;'[32] the holy is a '*value*, objective and ultimate'[33]— 'the "holy" will then be recognized as that which commands our respect'.[34] Further on, Otto describes it as 'a value, precious beyond all conceiving', and 'a might that has at the same time the supremest *right* to make the highest claim to service, and receives praise because it is in an absolute sense worthy to be praised'.[35]

It can be pointed out that Otto does not use the word 'ethical' when he speaks of this value; indeed he claims that it is not just an ethical value as such, 'not merely "perfect", or "beautiful" or "sublime", or "good" '.[36] Otto is all the time bringing out the 'extra' the 'something more' which he regards as belonging to the holy situation. He is constantly struggling against the tendency to identify the holy with the perfectly good; he will not allow the numinous to evaporate into the mere morally good. It seems to me that Oman should be more sympathetic towards

[30] *The Natural and the Supernatural* p. 59 (my italics).
[31] ibid. p. 61-62.
[32] *The idea of the Holy* p. 53.
[33] *The Idea of the Holy* p. 53.
[34] ibid. p. 53-4.
[35] ibid. p. 54.
[36] ibid. p. 53.

such an effort, for he himself wants to say something that is very similar. He argues that 'the sense of the holy is not mere moral reverence which follows a moral judgement. It is the sense of the Supernatural, and only becomes moral reverence because of the moral nature of this environment.'[37] When Oman states that 'the sacred, as here used, just means absoluteness of value, that which is of incomparable worth',[38] one wonders if the difference between his view and that of Otto is anything more than a matter of emphasis.

Both thinkers appeal to the Bible. Oman holds that 'the essential thing in the New Testament . . . is that the religious is always the ethical and the ethical always the religious'.[39] Otto refers to Isaiah's confession: 'I am a man of *unclean* lips and dwell among a people of unclean lips', and to that of Peter, who says 'Depart from me, for I am a *sinful* man, O Lord.'[40] Here we have a disvalue which goes beyond moral depreciation. These people have felt that they were '*sinful*', 'profane', and this is because they have seen themselves in the light of what Otto calls a 'quite special category of valuation and appraisement'.[41] This peculiar depreciation in terms of sinfulness indicates a correspondingly peculiar standard of judgement, and just as sinfulness is more than moral failure so also the standard by which one is judged sinful is more than a morally good one. But perhaps Otto goes too far when he says that this standard is *quite* distinct from the moral one.

Otto is by no means alone in wanting to differentiate between moral failure and sin, and between the corresponding moral goodness and holiness. H. H. Farmer says that sin is a 'specifically *religious* category'.[42] D. M. Baillie argues that when the soul is orientated towards God 'the consciousness of moral failure becomes something different: it becomes a sense of sin against God'.[43] Moreover, even Oman himself says that 'in the world of religion . . . mere morality should rejoice to lose itself, because it finds the love which is immeasurably more

---

[37] *The Natural and the Supernatural* p. 64.
[38] ibid. p. 65.
[39] *Journal of Theological Studies* Vol. XXV p. 285.
[40] *See Idea of the Holy* p. 52.
[41] ibid. p. 53.
[42] *The World and God* p. 184. (Nisbet, 1948).
[43] *God was in Christ* p. 165. (Faber, 1948).

than the fulfilling of its law'.[44] It is clear that Christian thinkers are not willing to equate sin and the corresponding state of virtue with the morally bad and morally good. Sin is not mere moral evil and Christian holiness is not mere moral goodness.

This question of the place of moral predicates in religion is touched upon by Professor G. E. Hughes in an article entitled 'An examination of the Argument from Theology to Ethics' which appeared in *Philosophy* Vol. XXII. He points out that the argument in question must presuppose the existence of God, and moreover, a good God, not necessarily good in the moral sense, 'still it is a *good* God that we require, although the goodness he possesses may be no more akin to moral goodness than say aesthetic goodness is'.[45] He adds : 'as to what we should call this theological value-characteristic there is little doubt; it is *holiness*'.[46] Later on he asks : 'is this property of holiness, which is recognized in religious experience, of a distinctly theological nature, or is it capable of analysis in non-theological terms?'[47] and Hughes himself is certain that 'the property in question *is* of a distinctively theological nature and is not capable of complete analysis in non-theological terms'.[48] So far, it seems that Hughes would side with Otto rather than Oman, but he shows how difficult he finds it to fall decisively for the one view rather than the other when he says of holiness : 'but whether it is wholly and exclusively theological, or on the other hand contains some *moral* elements is a question to which I find it particularly difficult to return any definite answer'.[49]

I should maintain that a moral element does come in here, and that if this is conceded it will be so much the less difficult to understand what holiness itself is. I have emphasized in my chapter on 'wholeness and holiness' that holiness is morality and *more*, but I also made a point of emphasizing that the morally good life was specially appropriate for harmonization with the divine personal 'whole'. I should now like to consider a particular moral theory, and to show how this could be modified by introducing the idea of a 'divine personal whole'. I

---

[44] *Grace and Personality* p. 313. (Cambridge, 1925).
[45] *Philosophy* Vol. XXII p. 12.   [46] ibid. p. 12.
[47] ibid. p. 12.   [48] ibid. p. 12-3.
[49] *ibid.* Vol. XXII p. 13.

shall then try to show how the modified theory fits in with the emphasis which we found in Otto, Oman and Hughes.

AN ETHICAL VIEW MODIFIED

R. M. Hare in his book *The Language of Morals* puts forward a thesis which makes moral principles in the last analysis a matter of personal choice. 'Ought'-sentences can only be verified by reference to a 'standard or set of principles which we have by our own decision accepted and made our own'.[50] At another point he says, 'we have to make our own decisions of principle'.[51] Value-judgements also come to the same thing in the end, for according to Hare 'to make a value-judgement is to make a decision of principle'.[52] Yet morality is not a purely subjective and arbitrary matter, for our decisions are made in the light of the objective facts of our environment. And further-more, they are not made independently of the decisions of other people, and it is obvious that many people agree to a small or greater degree on various principles. Indeed there are certain principles which have been held by many generations of people under very different circumstances. Thus, more often than not, what our decision amounts to is not a choice of new principles and new value-judgements, but a decision to accept or reject principles which have already secured a place of honour in the social environment into which we are born. To quote Hare, 'though principles are in the end built upon deci-sions of principle, the building is the work of many genera-tions'.[53]

Morality involves discovering, finding out something, learn-ing something. This aspect also comes out to some extent in Hare's book. He refers to the hypothetical case of a man who has to start the moral pilgrimage from the beginning, without the background of principles which one usually receives from the traditions one is born into, and says of him 'he will not be likely, unless he is a genius, to achieve many conclusions of im-portance, any more than the average boy, turned loose without

---

[50] *The Language of Morals* p. 78. (Oxford, 1952).
[51] ibid. p. 70. [52] ibid. p. 70.
[53] *ibid.* p.70.

instruction upon a desert island, or even in a laboratory, would be likely to make any of the major scientific discoveries'.[54] This element of discovery is also emphasized in a rather different way in Professor P. H. Nowell-Smith's book which is entitled *Ethics*. He holds that the sort of principles a man adopts depends in the end on his vision of 'the Good Life'[55] which is the man's own conception of the sort of world that he desires, so far as it rests with him, to create'.[56] This conception can change, and Nowell-Smith describes how this could come about. Perhaps a man 'meets someone whose character, conduct or arguments reveal to him new virtues that he has never even contemplated; or he may do something uncharacteristic and against his principles without choosing to do it and, in doing it, discover how good it is'.[56] He adds that, 'moral values, like other values, are sometimes discovered accidentally'.[56]

Neither Hare nor Nowell-Smith would hold that what we discover are facts with value-judgements already labelled on them. What is it then that we discover or find? A very helpful example, taken from Hare's book, is that of discovering the principles of good driving. They may be given to us by a B.S.M. instructor but we cannot properly appreciate the value of many of the prescriptions involved except through the actual experience of driving. It is then that we decide for the principles and accept them as our own, and we do this because we find that they work. Collisions are avoided by giving certain signals, therefore we accept, and decide for, the giving of such signals as a principle of our driving, and we decide at the same time that good driving will be driving which incorporates the giving of those signals. What we discover are the factors to which we will subsequently refer in giving reasons for calling a certain sample of driving 'good', or the conditions which elicit from us the appropriate value-judgement.

Morality one might say is a matter of learning to live. What we discover in morality are the conditions which elicit from us a valuation of certain acts or forms of behaviour as 'good'. In other words, we discover the circumstances in the light of which we decide to accept or reject certain principles of action.

[54] *The Language of Morals* p. 76.   [55] *Ethics* p. 313. (Penguin, 1954).
[56] *ibid.* p. 313.

An important part of what morality involves is an ever wider knowledge and understanding of the facts and conditions of living in our world.

There is, however, another equally important aspect which must be considered. This I can best bring out by saying that there is a sense in which we discover *ourselves* in the moral pilgrimage. It is of course psychologically true that we often feel as though we suddenly came upon ourselves from around a corner. One may say 'I suddenly found myself in a heated argument with the main speaker', and if one is of a reticent disposition he might well add, 'I never knew I could be so brave before'. We sometimes do genuinely surprise ourselves, and this is an indication of something deeper and more important. There are certain convictions and valuations in our lives that do not show up until we are thrown into the circumstances that evoke an expression of them. One might be asked: 'Are you an abolitionist?' and the reply might be 'I don't really know whether I am or not', but the occurrence of certain local incidents which were of peculiar interest to the person in question might bring him to say 'now I'm certain of it—I can never be an abolitionist'. Still, further circumstances might cause him to change his mind again, and he will then have learnt something about the transitoriness of his own feelings and the need for a firmer basis for his convictions.

Yet, it is not the case that when I find myself I discover obscure, ghostly ingredients in the hidden recesses of my character. That picture does not do full justice to the circumstances. For through my decisions I, in a sense, *make* myself, and what I discover is therefore not something which was previously hidden away, but something that only came into being through my very decision itself. It is partly at any rate through decision at the moral-principle level that a man becomes what he is. There are passages in *Language and Morals* which suggest that Hare thought this too. He agrees with the subjectivist to the extent that 'if I refuse to make my own decisions, I am, in merely copying my fathers, showing myself a lesser man than they; for whereas they must have initiated, I shall be merely accepting'. The plea of the subjectivist, who emphasizes the importance of decision is, according to Hare, 'the plea of the

adolescent who wants to be an adult'.[57] The implication surely
is that a man grows and in a sense makes himself through decisions. On this point, the existentialists have something to teach
us, even though we may not accept, or agree with, their whole
development of the theme. I would not want to suggest that
what is created through decision is a shadowy 'ghost in the
machine' called a character, though I do not commit myself to
the view that it is all only a matter of behaviour and disposi-
tions either. I only wish to point out that whatever we mean
by a 'person', he is built up in part at least through his own
decisions.

Having given these sketchy indications of what seems to me
to be a plausible ethical view, I must now relate it to the notion
of 'divine personal whole', that is, 'God'. This will involve using
the terms 'knowledge', 'will' and 'decision' of God. It can be
very misleading to say that God 'knows' anything, since this
almost inevitably implies that his knowledge is comparable to
ours. But the difference between God's knowledge and our own
is vast, for it is said that he is 'omniscient'. This should not be
taken to imply simply a vast sum of knowledge similar to, only
greater than, that which we already possess. Knowledge at the
level of omniscience would not be simply greater in amount
than what we human beings possess but also vastly different in
character and nature. We just cannot imagine what it would
be like; to grasp what this means is intimately tied up with
grasping what is meant by 'God' or any of the other terms
which I have mentioned as being more or less equivalent to it.
'Omniscience' should be given a logical status similar to these.

Religious believers also speak of God as having a *will*—for
instance, in the words of The Lord's Prayer 'Thy will be done.'
But this again is not an ordinary will and, indeed, we sometimes
indicate this by referring to it as a *holy* will. To know what is
meant by 'will' here would involve knowing what is meant by
'God' or 'divine personal whole' or 'holy power', and this is just
another pointer to the central importance of this question of
how to understand these latter terms. Now, if we bear in mind
the extraordinary significance of the terms 'omniscient' and
'divine will' or 'holy will', I think we can venture to say that

[57] *The Language of Morals* p. 77.

the 'divine person' has 'principles', which correspond in some way to our moral principles. We might call them 'God's holy laws'. We cannot comprehend them as we comprehend our own moral principles, but we can think of them as being an expression of God's 'will' or ultimate 'decision', a 'will' which is intimately associated with divine 'omniscience'. If we were to use the word 'know' in connection with this 'divine person' at all, then we should say that the 'divine person' 'knows' himself as fully as he 'knows' everything else; and he will certainly never be surprised in himself, neither is he in process of creating himself. Thus this 'divine person' would be the *final* value-decider; the principles which would be an expression of his will would be *ultimate*. They would be 'moral' principles of a very special kind in that they were not the expression of an ordinary will of a human being, but of an extraordinary will, a 'will' which did not operate in the light of ordinary knowledge but in the light of 'omniscience'.

Now if it did make sense to talk of such a 'divine person' then it seems to me that it would also make sense to speak of the human sphere of moral behaviour in a way which is very different from the account given above. We could now speak of the search for the highest moral principles as a search for the 'will' of the 'divine person', and to know the ultimate moral principles would be to know that 'will'. Similarly, the attempt to live a good moral life could be seen as an attempt to do the 'will' of the 'divine' person, and to decide in accordance with his 'will'. Also, since the 'divine person's' value-decision is an expression of his person, to know his decisions is also to know him. And similarly to do his 'will' is to become like him, to become what he is. Our creating of ourselves through decisions of moral principles could now be seen as growth after the likeness and image of the 'divine person'. I must emphasize that this does not imply that to become morally good means, *by definition*, becoming like the 'divine person'. It would simply be a fact that in becoming morally good we should also be getting more like the 'divine person', and this would be so in virtue of the conditions already described.

THE INTERRELATION OF HOLINESS AND GOODNESS

Let us look again, in the light of the view which I have just developed, at what Oman says about holiness and the Supernatural.

On the view which I have just developed we can say that the character of the Supernatural is given in his choice, and since he chooses the ultimate value there is a point in claiming that the Supernatural has for us absolute value and that this supernatural being should be considered as having incomparable worth. In this light we can see the nature of Oman's claim that the supreme task of human progress has been 'to discover the true sacred',[58] the sacred which is 'absoluteness of value, that which is of incomparable worth'.[59] Our picture does justice to Oman's belief that morality takes on a new meaning in the religious setting; it becomes 'the righteousness which is no longer a rule, but the infinite requirement of love, (it) changes from a code into an inspiration which transforms the measurelessness of duty into the measurelessness of faith, the measurelessness of what God means and will accomplish',[60] and in the light of the same picture we can see the point of saying that *God's will alone is the measure and the end of our duty*'.[61] This last phrase should not be interpreted analytically, for 'such a God is wholly without arbitrariness' and 'conscience cannot be too independent in judging of His righteousness'.[62] Above all, our picture shows how there are for religious thinkers two possible views of morality, the one a 'morality of imperatives',[63] and the other a 'profounder morality'.[64]

Similarly, we can see why Vincent Taylor, in his book *Forgiveness and Reconciliation*, should want to hold that 'in Christianity there are no ethical aims which are not at the same time spiritual, and there are no spiritual ideals which are not also ethical'.[65] A reading of Taylor's chapter on 'Sanctification' in

[58] *Science, Religion and Reality* p. 297.
[59] *The Natural and the Supernatural* p. 65.
[60] *Grace and Personality* p. 103-4. (Cambridge, 1925).
[61] ibid. p. 236.   [62] ibid. p. 107.
[63] *Grace and Personality* p. 235.   [64] ibid. p. 112.
[65] *Forgiveness and Reconciliation* p. 145. (Macmillan, 1948).

the book just mentioned above shows how different from a
non-Christian conception of ethics the Christian ethic is. The
Christian ethical progress is at the same time a 'life moving
towards ethical and spiritual *perfection*'.[66] The ideal is a state
of '*sinless* perfection', and this ideal is also described as being
the '*vision* of God',[66] and '*perfect* love'.[66] Indeed this insistence
upon love as being the essence of God's will is one of the most
prominent features of Christian teaching, and the ultimate
Christian demand seems to be that we should be loving. Anders
Nygren claims this in no indefinite terms when he says that 'the
idea of Agape is not merely a fundamental idea of Christianity,
but *the* fundamental idea *par excellence*. The idea of Agape is
a new creation of Christianity. It sets its mark on the whole of
Christianity. Without it nothing that is Christian would be
Christian.'[67]

What happens in the case of those who emphasize the
ethical nature of God, and of the ethical nature of the process
of sanctification, is that they modify their use of the words
'ethics' or 'morals' beyond the secular or purely philosophical
use, by the addition of such qualifying terms as 'perfect',
'absolute', 'incomparable'. It then becomes obvious that these
thinkers wish to imply something more by those terms than
what they convey in their ordinary contexts. The word 'love' is
specially useful since it has a moral connotation while at the
same time rising above the level of ordinary moral discourse.

Turning again to Hughes's remarks in the aforementioned
article, it will be seen that they also fit in with the same ethical
picture. Since he is not sure whether holiness is exclusively
theological or contains some moral elements, he considers both
possibilities in the working out of his argument from theology
to ethics, but only the former case need occupy us now, for
Hughes does think that there definitely is an aspect of the
worthiness of God which cannot be analysed in *non*-theological
terms, and it is in this respect that he differs from such thinkers
as Oman. Hughes argues that if there is a God who possesses
this unique holy worthiness, then 'the claim which he legiti-
mately makes upon us in virtue of that holiness is, . . . a

[66]*Forgiveness and Reconciliation* p. 155 (my italics).
[67] *Agape and Eros* Part I p. 32. (S.P.C.K., 1932).

complete and all-embracing claim to that which at a lower level we are content to call our "respect", but which at this level we can more appropriately call our "devotion" or "love".[68] In view of the ethical picture I sketched it would be natural to speak of 'respecting' the principles I decide upon as my ultimate moral valuations, and it would not be at all inappropriate to speak of someone's 'respecting' his own person by observing those principles. The least, but also the most, such moral principles would deserve would be respect. Such respect is the fitting attitude towards someone who is conscientious but not infallible or without room for improvement. But what if the principle or person was infallible, beyond possibility of correction? Then, such words as Hughes chooses would be fitting. 'Devotion', 'love' become the appropriate terms.

Hughes holds that the claims of God's supreme goodness (not mere ethical goodness) upon us are claims 'not only on certain aspects of our selves and our activities, but on our *whole* selves'.[69] This too would be natural on the view that I presented. If God is 'all-knowing', and his value-judgements thereby ultimate, then these are the value-judgements that every one of us might in the last resort be expected to make his own, and moreover these should have precedence over any other principles that govern our life; they should be our basic principles. And if we make ourselves, in a sense, through our decisions, then the claim is really a claim upon our whole person. Thus we could agree with Hughes that 'to love God fully, . . . to give him the complete devotion which is his due, is a matter not merely of feeling certain emotions towards him or of doing certain actions, but of being a certain kind of person'.[70]

Finally, Hughes's distinction between moral wrong and sin would also be valid on the view I expounded, sin being the choice of principles which are at variance with God's will, and therefore implying a certain state of the person—a state of sin. When seen against the moral view that I have given, Hughes comes very near to the position of Oman and both are supported by such works of Biblical exegesis as that of sanctification given by Vincent Taylor. It seems that where Hughes

---

[68] *Philosophy* Vol. XXII p. 17.   [69] *ibid.* p. 18.
[70] ibid. p. 18.

differs from such thinkers as Oman is in reserving the word 'holiness', and rejecting the term 'moral value', when speaking of that which Oman is content to call 'absolute value', 'incomparable worth', the 'ethical sacred'.

Otto's position is also quite close to all these thinkers in the last analysis. He brought out the emphasis, which Hughes echoes, on the *sui generis* character of holiness, denying that it is moral worth of any degree, yet coming round in the end to a doctrine of schematism which allows him to describe God as possessing the attributes of created spirit in an absolute degree. 'Human love,' says Otto, 'is relative, admitting of degrees, and it is the same with human knowledge and human goodness,' but 'God's love and knowledge and goodness, on the other hand, and all else that can be asserted of Him in conceptual terms, are formally absolute.'[71] By way of schematism, so it would seem, Otto can cross over to speak in the same terms as Oman. The difference again is that the one denies that any moral valuation applies to God in a straightforward way (only via schematism), the other thinks it does, so long as the valuation is made absolute. What stands out from the discussion of the present chapter is that yet one more approach to our question, namely the approach via the ethical associations of holiness, has brought us to the notion of an extraordinary, supernatural 'person'. We have seen how very closely holiness is associated with ethical notions in the writings of different religious thinkers, and we have seen how each ofthe se writers has in his own way emphasized that holiness is more than mere moral goodness. I have tried to show how a contemporary view of ethics might be adapted to incorporate harmoniously the different emphases of these writers. This was done by introducing again the notion of an extraordinary 'person' who might well be identified with the Christian God.

Both Nowell-Smith and Hare have emphasized that in the last resort it is for the person himself to say what his ultimate values are, and that he can come to adopt different evaluative principles as he gains in experience. I suggest that it is not inconceivable that there should be an omniscient being who is not in the position of a learner starting from ignorance, a

[71] *The Idea of the Holy* p. 145.

person for whom there would be nothing to gain by experience, and whose value judgements would therefore be unalterable. If my suggestion holds, then we could also have that objectivity in moral standards after which some moral philosophers have hankered, and that without departing radically from such views as those of Hare and Nowell-Smith. The concept of a final value-decider leads us to the idea of an absolute standard of moral goodness which is, I suggest, what religious believers have in mind when they speak, in ethical contexts, of holiness. This development of the contemporary ethical view just mentioned makes clear both the affinity between holiness and moral goodness which makes it plausible to speak of the one in connection with the other, and also the difference between them which justifies us in saying that holiness is moral goodness and *more*.

The earlier approaches, via the associations of 'holiness' with 'fear', 'physical power', 'will-power', 'love' 'wholeness' and 'separatedness', all lead to this same notion of an extraordinary 'person'. It should be clear by now that this notion is of crucial importance if we are to understand what is meant by holiness. If this notion turned out to be spurious then I should have to conclude my account of holiness by showing that the word belongs to the language of primitive religion comprising much superstition and myth. The superstitious elements would be such that no moderately sophisticated person placed in the context of modern civilization could include them in his pattern of beliefs. The mythical elements would be equally otiose, though some might want to preserve them as reinforcements of moral principles. It is not difficult to imagine how my discussion of fear, holy power, separatedness, wholeness and moral goodness could be reinterpreted and developed in this direction. For instance, if the notion of an extraordinary person turned out to be spurious then the fear of the holy which I considered earlier on would be purely superstitious. We should have to say that there was nothing more behind the Hebrew's fear of touching the ark than sheer ignorance, and that there was no room at all for a fear that was in any way comparable to it in the life of a present-day citizen. One would not need to have any *more* qualms about desecrating an altar than about interfering with some one else's property. In both cases there would be contravention of moral and property laws, but nothing *more* would have been done which should give cause for any *special* worry on a religious count. Any such further worry would be entirely due to superstition; it would be based upon fear of reprisal by a being or spirit which simply did not exist at all.

If, however, this notion of an extraordinary 'person' is as respectable and significant as many present-day religious believers think it is, then my account could conclude on a very different note, and the conclusion would harmonize reasonably well with the beliefs and practice of Hebrew and Christian religion. Thus the development of my discussion at this stage must turn on the meaningfulness or otherwise of the notion of an extraordinary 'divine person'. Not only has my discussion led us to this point, but this is precisely what one should expect in view of the intimate logical tie-up that exists between the notions of holiness, God and personality in Hebrew and Christian literature including the Bible itself. I will show the intimacy of this connection by reference to Old and New Testament and subsequent Christian literature before going on to consider the significance of the notion of an extraordinary 'divine person'.

CHAPTER IX

'HOLINESS', 'GOD'
AND 'DIVINE PERSONALITY'

ONE important point that emerges from the discussion in each
of my previous chapters is that the words 'holiness', 'God' and
'divine person' have close logical associations within theistic
language. The fear of, and respect for, holiness turned out to
be a fear of, and respect for a 'divine person', that is, God. The
power which is present in holy-situations, the power of creation, life, and love was seen to be best understood as an extraordinary personal power, the power of the Holy Ghost, the
power of God himself. We saw that the wholeness which is
holiness is a personal wholeness, and the question of separatedness led us to the same conclusion. Finally, when a moral situation is also a holy one, then the ultimate authority is a 'divine
person', God. A holy-situation is almost invariably a God-situa-
tion, and a situation in which we want to speak of a 'divine
person'. The upshot seems to be that there is a very strong and
close logical link between the terms 'God', 'holiness' and 'divine
person', and we shall see that they can indeed be used interchangeably in many contexts.

I now wish to bring out further, by reference to Biblical and
theological literature, the logical kinship of these terms. I shall,
in the first place, attempt to exemplify the very close kinship
that exists between the words 'holy' and 'holiness' on the one
hand, and the word 'God' on the other, as these words are used
by Hebrew and Christian believers. So close is the kinship that
one may say that holiness is the very essence of God, so that
God is sometimes called 'holiness'. Further, it follows that talk
about God provides the paradigm use of the words 'holy' and
'holiness'; other people and various objects will only be called
'holy' in virtue of their relationship with him. It is rather as
though one had coined the word 'socratiness' to refer to the
essential character of the man Socrates, and in such circum-

stances Socrates would of course provide the paradigm case of socratiness. The only way to explain what was meant by 'socratiness' would be by reference to the word 'Socrates' from which it was derived. The logical kinship between the words 'holy', 'holiness' and 'God' is, I suggest as close as this, and if so the upshot is that in order to know more about what 'holiness' means we shall have to get some light on the meaning of the word 'God'. My first task then will be to substantiate this suggestion by reference to Biblical and theological literature.

Secondly, I wish to show the very close logical kinship that exists between the word 'God' and the word 'person', and especially 'divine person'. I have just suggested above that the question: what is meant by 'holiness'? leads to the further question: what is meant by 'God'? rather as the question: what do you mean by 'socratiness'? would in my invented example lead to the question: what do you mean by 'Socrates'? We would answer this latter question by pointing out that 'Socrates' functions as the name of a person, and I hope to show that in religious discourse the word 'God' too is used to refer to a person, but the two cases are not quite parallel however, for God is not an ordinary person who could be described and identified as we can describe and identify Socrates. God is an extraordinary 'person', a supernatural 'person', a divine 'person', and my second task in this chapter will be to establish this point by reference to Biblical and Christian theological literature. Thus we are brought round again to the point which I have emphasized from the beginning, namely, the central and crucial importance of this notion of an extraordinary, divine 'person' for our understanding of holiness. Whichever way we look at it, to understand what 'holiness' means involves understanding what is meant by 'divine person' and it is to this crucial question that I will address myself in the next chapter.

A. THE LOGICAL KINSHIP BETWEEN 'GOD', 'HOLY' AND 'HOLINESS'

Beginning with Biblical evidence, we find Amos using the words 'Jehovah' and 'holiness' as though they were interchangeable. We read in Amos 4/2 that 'the Lord God hath sworn by his holiness', but in 6/8 the reading is 'the Lord God hath sworn by himself', and the obvious implication is that Jehovah, the Lord God, is himself holiness so far as the prophet is concerned. The book of Isaiah provides instances which betray very much the same outlook. God is often called the 'Holy One' (e.g. Is. 40/25, 55/5); we are specifically told that his 'name is holy' (Is. 57/15), and it should be remembered that for the Hebrew a name was more or less 'an equivalent of the "personality" or "character" or nature of the person or thing named'.[1] The name publicized the person, and it is obvious that the terms 'Yahweh' and 'Holy One' publicized the same person in Hebrew literature. The prophet Habakkuk, in his prayer, glorifies God saying:

'God came from Teman,

And the Holy One from mount Paran'. (Hab. 3/3),

thus implying that for him too holiness was the essence of God. On the prophetical view holiness is, as Gray says in his volume on Isaiah, 'the essential nature of deity'.[2] God is holiness itself. To say that he is holy is not therefore to describe him but to emphasize that he is the one he is. When it is said that God is holy, 'what is asserted is not anything about His character, but simply His supreme Godhead'.[3] Skinner therefore can well say in the article from which I have just quoted: 'the question as to the contents of the idea of divine holiness thus resolves itself into the larger question of the conception of Godhead by which religious practice and devotion were ruled'.[4] It should be noted here that Skinner makes it clear that the holiness in question is divine holiness; holiness is attributed to places, things and people, but only in a derivative sense as we shall see. When mention is made of *God's* holiness it seems that the reference is simply to his divine nature as such. J. E. Fison emphasizes this same point, saying that *qodesh* 'indicates a relation to Yahweh, and so close is that relation that A. B. Davidson can describe the word, holy, when combined with the word, God, as "a mere otiose epithet" '.[5]

---

[1] *Hasting's Dictionary of the Bible* Vol. III p. 478b. (T. & T. Clarke, 1904).
[2] *International Critical Commentary Isaiah* p. lxxxix. (T. & T. Clarke, 1928).
[3] *Hasting's Dictionary of the Bible* Vol. II p. 396b.
[4] ibid. p. 397a.   [5] *The Blessing of the Holy Spirit* p. 43.

It is not, however, right to say that 'holy', when combined with 'God', is 'a mere otiose epithet' for it should still be remembered that by its very emphasis upon the fact that God is who he is, it also serves the negative purpose of emphasizing that this God is not to be confused with any other. However many other gods there might be Yahweh was not of their number; he stood alone and aloft as the Holy One of Israel. When Skinner says that 'holy' does not tell us anything about God's character, it will be remembered that he very fittingly adds that it was the '*supreme* Godhead' that was asserted (vid. supra.). Various nations had their own deities whom they could call 'god' or 'God', but one way of making sure that Yahweh was not confused with any of these was to insert the word 'holy' before his name. It now becomes still clearer that to know what holiness means involves more than just enquiring into some general notion of deity, or into the nature of any god we like to choose; it means that we have to ask what is meant by the 'God' of Hebrew and Christian thought, in other words, the '*holy* God', of whom it was said : 'there is none holy as Yahweh, for there is none beside thee' (I Sam. 2/2), and of whom Deutero-Isaiah asks : 'To whom then will ye liken me, that I should be equal to him? saith the Holy One' (Is. 40/25). As Ringgren comments—'the Holy One is the incomparable One'.[6]

Another way of showing that to know what holiness means involves knowing what the Hebrews and Christians mean by 'God' is by drawing attention to the difference between 'holy' as applied to God and the same word as applied to places, people and things. God is holy in himself and independently of his relation to anything or anyone else, whereas they all derive their holiness from him. I quote Ringgren once more : 'no thing, or person is holy in itself, but becomes holy when it is placed in relation to God'.[7] Priests, Levites and prophets could be holy, but never in their own right nor in virtue of their connection with anything other than God himself,—'not by reason of their associations with a shrine, but because of their unique relation-

---

[6] *The Prophetical Conception of Holiness* p. 27.
[7] ibid. p. 9.

ship with Yahweh'.[8] God alone is essentially and necessarily holy; other people, and things and places can only become holy in virtue of their relationship to God.

This view is found in the Early Christian Church no less than in Old Testament Hebrew circles. G. L. Prestige, in his book *God in Patristic Thought*, considers the use of the word 'hagiasma' and other cognates of 'hagios' as used by various early Christian Fathers, and comes to the following conclusion: 'in all the cases which have been illustrated it is plain that the true and ultimate source of holiness is God, and that all the other objects to which it is ascribed derive such holiness as they possess by participation from that primal fount'.[9] Firmilian's phrase 'deifying holiness'[10] might well be adduced in support of what Prestige tells us and what I have been claiming when, for instance, I said that the holiness of things, places, and people consists in their incorporation into the 'divine whole'. If holiness is God himself then its effect upon man might not at all inappropriately be called a process of deifying. The person upon whom the spirit of God operates in this way becomes holy in so far as he becomes somewhat like God himself—a holy man is often called a godly man; holiness is Godliness.

This view of holiness is still held in our own time. Paul Tillich speaks for protestantism as follows: 'since to it God alone is holy in himself . . . every man and everything and every group is profane in itself and is sacred only in so far as it becomes a symbol of the divine holiness'.[11] One might question Tillich's use of the word 'symbol' here but if it be allowed that a symbol sometimes participates in the thing it symbolizes,[12] then one could hold that the Christian himself can symbolize God's holiness in so far as such holiness is to some degree present in his life through his participation in God's life through the salvation of Christ. But it is also true that the relation be-

---

[8] *The Blessing of the Holy Spirit* p. 51.
[9] *God in Patristic Thought* p. 24. (Heinemann, 1936).
[10] Quoted in *Church-Life and Church-Order* p. 68 by J. V. Bartlett (Blackwell, 1943).
[11] *The Protestant Era* p. 230.
[12] This is what H. H. Farmer calls an 'intrinsic symbol'. He says: 'an intrinsic or expressive symbol is one which is organically related to, and sustained by, the wider and deeper reality which it represents' (*The World and God* p. 74).

tween God and that which is called holy is often much more remote than this, and this is particularly so in the case of objects and places that are called holy. It is not that there is any of God's holiness residing in these things at all, or that they are like God. They are called holy because of their associations with God's presence, just as a seaside resort is called healthy only because people who live or stay there get good health. People are sometimes called 'holy' when their relation to God is of this secondary type; for instance a man in holy orders might be called 'holy' even though he might in point of fact turn out to be ungodly so far as his person and character go.

It is a relation, close or remote, to God that justifies calling anything or anybody 'holy', and not any quality, characteristic, or nontheistic relation. God on the other hand is holy purely in virtue of the fact that he is the one unique God that he is. Thus, to understand what is meant when people, places and objects are called holy involves tracing their relationship to God, but to understand what 'holiness' means when used of God himself involves an enquiry into the very meaning of the word 'God' itself. It is, I suggest, a word whose logical behaviour, however extraordinary, has close affinities with the word 'person'. I now propose to justify this claim.

B. IS THE HEBREW AND CHRISTIAN GOD A PERSONAL GOD?

In the second creation narrative given in Gen. 2/4ff. we find an anthropomorphic conception of God which suggests that he was very much like any ordinary person except that he had greater powers. This God was a maker rather than a creator; it seems that he worked with his hands, and would walk in the garden in the cool of the day. Yet, obviously, the Hebrew could set this story alongside another which is very different in character, namely the account that we have in Gen. 1-2/4. As Oesterley and Robinson say: 'there is no longer any suggestion of a human frame or of mechanical measures for the construction of the Universe; God speaks, and it is done'. The phrase 'God said' could be more faithfully represented by saying 'God *willed'.*[13] God is still thought of as being a person in this more sophisticated narrative, but it is obvious here that he is not an ordinary person with hands and feet and so forth. The setting of the two narratives side by side shows that the Hebrew did not put any special emphasis on the anthropomorphic descriptions of God. The story in Gen. 2/4ff. could be accepted because the Hebrew never ceased to think of God as being a person, but the later story of Gen. 1-2/4 shows how emphasis shifted more towards the *extraordinary* character of this person.

The name 'Yahweh' invariably figures in Hebrew literature as the name of a person. He is a God who 'repented' and was 'grieved' (Gen. 6/6), who 'heard' his people's groaning and 'remembered' his covenant (Ex. 2/24), and whose 'anger' was kindled when the Israelites disobeyed him (Judges 10/7); he 'spake' unto Moses (Ex. 7/8), 'called' Samuel (I Sam. 3/4). Isaiah 'heard the voice of the Lord' (Is. 6/8), and the usual introductory phrase of a prophetic utterance was: 'thus saith the Lord' (Ez. 5/5 et. al.). But Yahweh was an extraordinary sort of person altogether. As I have already pointed out, the only visible signs of his presence were cloud or smoke, and his voice was sometimes thunder, and sometimes the voice of gentle stillness. To sum up in the words of Professor T. H. Robinson, the Old Testament 'could conceive of God only as a person, differing in many ways from human persons, but still a person'.[14] Professor Porteous maintains that revelation would not be possible unless God were in some sense a person: 'the possibility that God should reveal Himself to men at all is grounded in the fact that man was created in the likeness of God and that there is, therefore, a relationship of analogy between the divine and the human personality'.[15] I have no reason to doubt that the views of these two Old Testament scholars are fairly representative on the points in question.

God is still spoken of as though he were a person in the New Testament, the favourite term for him there being 'Father' (John Ch. 14, Math 6/9). In the Old Testament God had sym-

---

[13] *Hebrew Religion* p. 371.
[14] *The Old Testament and Modern Study* p. 348.
[15] ibid. p. 335.

bolic figures as his representatives on earth, 'the patriarch-leader, the saviour-hero and the prophet-reformer' and in post-Restoration days 'the priest-King and the teacher-lawgiver',[16] but in the New Testament we meet a representative who is pre-eminent amongst all others in that he claims to be the Son of God and in knowing whom we also know the Father himself (John 14/9). The claim that Jesus Christ is the perfect revelation of God would seem to reinforce in no uncertain manner the claim that God is a person, for Christ himself was certainly a person. Christ would seem to be even a historical person, that is, a person in the straightforward undisputed sense in which any human being is a person. He walked amongst, spoke to, and mixed in with, the residents of Galilee. Was it the case then that God had at last walked out of his hiding-place so that people could now see the colour of his eyes and measure his height?

Now when Jesus asked his disciples for the verdict of the people upon himself (Math. 16/13f. Mk. 8/27f. Lk. 9/18f.) he received a variety of answers—John the Baptist, Elijah, one of the prophets. Evidently, many thought him an exceptional, though not an unique, person. But when the question was put to the disciples themselves, Simon Peter answered 'Thou art the Christ' (Mk. 8/29), and whether Jesus actually uttered the response given in Matt. 16/17 or not, the words certainly express the Christian belief that 'the revelation is from heaven and not of men'.[17] Jesus's purported reply included the following words: 'for flesh and blood hath not revealed it unto thee by my Father which is in heaven' (Matt. 16/17). It was not flesh and blood, not eyes or ears, that could have appreciated the revelatory character of Jesus, and it was not simply as flesh and blood—a body with certain characteristic features and manifesting certain forms of behaviour—that Jesus revealed God. Again, it was not at the first moment of acquaintance that the woman of Samaria saw that Jesus was no ordinary person (John Ch. 4); and the blind man of whose cure we are told in John Ch. 9 saw Jesus first as a man (v. 11), then as a prophet (v. 17), but only on his third interrogation did he recognize

[16] *Christianity and Symbolism* p. 129.
[17] *The Sayings of Jesus* by T. W. Manson p. 204. (S.C.M. Press, 1949).

Jesus as the Son of God (v. 35-38). One could see Jesus, listen to him, observe his behaviour, and yet fail to recognize him as the Son of God. Thus, in the New Testament, as in the Old Testament, God is presented as a person, though not an ordinary person who is to be classified with other persons, even if those others were prophets.

The Old and the New Testament present God to us as a person, but the word 'person' itself is not to be found until we come to the context of Christian theistic discussion within the early church. Ironically enough, when the word did come into use it was in connection with the fiercest arguments concerning Trinitarian doctrine, arguments which made it impossible to ascribe personality to God except at the risk of being misunderstood. In the long run the preponderance of opinion in the Christian Church favoured a restriction of the use of the word 'person' to refer to one member of the Trinity as distinct from the other two. According to C. C. J. Webb, 'it was only to express that which distinguished one from another of the members of the Trinity acknowledged by the Christian Church to exist within the unity of the Godhead that the word 'Person' was regularly employed in theology down to the period of the Reformation'.[18] Yet, since the orthodox have persistently emphasized the unity of the three Persons in the one Godhead, the ascription of personality to the three members individually cannot be construed as a denial that God himself is personal. It was not the case that the Early Fathers' conception of God had changed so radically that the Hebrew personal element was lost and gave place to a new impersonal conception. God was still thought of as personal, but certain developments in the history of the terms 'προσωπον' and 'persona' prevented their being used in the Old Testament sense of the divine personality of God. These terms are very close together in meaning, and are the fore-runners of the present-day English 'person'. They did not, however, in the early period of Church history carry the meaning which the English word 'person' carries today. 'Persona' meant first an actor's mask, then, to

---

[18] *God and Personality* p. 67-8. (Allen & Unwin, 1918). A reluctance to use the word 'person' of God is evident in the writings of Berkeley for instance. See *Philosophical Commentaries Section* 713 and 715. (Nelson, 1948).

quote Bethune-Baker, 'by an easy transition, the part the actor plays, which is represented by his mask; then, any part or rôle assumed by any one without regard to its duration. Secondly, it is the *condicio, status, munus* which anyone has among men in general, and in particular in civil life. And so it is the man himself as far as he has this or that *persona*.'[19] Bethune-Baker further tells us that 'the history of προσωπον is similar, as to its primary uses, to that of *persona*'.[20] Indeed, C. C. J. Webb assures us that 'the term προσωπον "even more than *persona*" suggests "a mere aspect or *rôle*".'[21] Sabellius made use of the word in this sense to emphasize his view that the three 'persons' of the Trinity were simply three *phases* under which the one divine essence reveals itself. Once the word had been used in this way, it could not then be used to signify the more permanent and deeper personal nature of God. As Bethune-Baker succinctly puts it; 'Sabellius stole the word away'.[22] This does not, however, mean that the personal nature of God is overlooked in the doctrine of the Trinity. Professor Farmer, for one, is convinced that it 'is a vigorous assertion that . . . personality and personal relationship are constitutive of the divine being'.[23]

Long after the Trinitarian controversies had died down, as late as the end of the eighteenth century, the term 'personality of God' came into currency. To borrow the words of C. C. J. Webb once more, 'accordingly we find Schleiermacher in the last year of the eighteenth century referring to it as an expression familiar to his hearers and Paley in the third year of the nineteenth devoting a chapter of his *Natural Theology* to the "Personality of the Deity" '.[24] By the early part of the present century Webb could say that it is 'taken for granted nowadays that the Personality of God is a principal tenet of Christianity',[25] and it is worth noting that Webb's own view is that 'the recognition of Personality in God imparts to religious ideas generally

---

[19] *The Early History of Christian Doctrine* p. 233.
[20] ibid. p. 234.
[21] *God and Personality* p. 46.
[22] *The Early History of Christian Doctrine* p. 235.
[23] *Revelation and Religion* p. 59.
[24] *God and Personality* p. 65.
[25] *God and Personality* p. 61.

an increase of intelligibility and of ethical significance'.[26] Some religious thinkers are more emphatic in their insistence upon the personal nature of God. John Macmurray, in his contribution to the volume entitled *Adventure—the Faith of Science and the Science of Faith*, insists that 'there can be no question of an impersonal God'. 'The phrase is,' he says, 'a contradiction in terms.'[27] L. E. Elliot-Binns, discussing the theological thought in England in the latter half of the nineteenth century says that 'personality therefore is the least inadequate symbol by means of which we can represent God'.[28] Professor H. H. Farmer is constantly emphasizing that God is personal, and he begins the introduction to *The World and God* by affirming that 'the conviction that God is personal, and deals personally with men and women, lies at the heart of Christian experience and thought'.[29]

Having said all this, I must emphasize how important it is that we should bear in mind that the claim that God is personal nearly always involves a certain qualifier which is to the effect that God is not an ordinary person, and this is expressed in various ways by different religious thinkers. One popular way of doing this is to insist that God is a 'perfect' or 'complete' person by contrast with whom all human beings are imperfect or incomplete. This terminology can be traced back to Lotze, who, in his *Gründzuge der Religionsphilosophie*, described God as a person who is not bounded by any reality which is outside of, or independent of, himself. It has been argued that an infinite, unlimited, being such as this could not properly be called a person, but Lotze argued that on the contrary it is finite, limited personality, such as we human beings possess, which is incomplete and imperfect. It is only the infinite and unlimited personality of God that is complete and perfect. 'Complete personality can only be in God, while to man can belong but a weak and faint copy thereof.'[30] Baron von Hugel agrees with Lotze on this point in the *Essays and Addresses on*

---

[26] *God and Personality* p. 259.
[27] *Adventure* p. 183. (Macmillan, 1927).
[28] *English Thought 1860-1900—The Theological Aspect* p. 235. (Longmans, 1956).
[29] *The World and God* p. 1.
[30] *The Philosophy of Religion* p. 72. (ed. F. C. Conybeare, 1892).

the Philosophy of Religion,[31] and others have since made use of the same terminology. F. R. Tennant held that theism can allow 'that human personality is but "a pale copy" of divine personality, or that God is the only perfect Person'.[32] 'We must suppose,' says W. R. Matthews, 'the Divine Experience to be the sole example of personality in its completeness.'[33] This is also John Baillie's view when he maintains that 'he who knows the poverty of his own personality knows it only because there has first been revealed to him the perfect personality of God'.[34]

Tennant suggests another way of qualifying the word 'person' in order to show that God is not just like any other person. Tennant is quite convinced that God is not impersonal, yet he is afraid that the word 'person' might misrepresent God by suggesting too close a likeness between him and ordinary human beings, so Tennant suggests that we should call God 'supra-personal'.[35] Bradley expresses a somewhat similar view with regard to the Absolute. He holds that 'if the term "personal" is to bear anything like its ordinary sense, assuredly the Absolute is not merely personal'.[36] He adds that 'it is not personal, because it is personal and more. It is, in a word, super-personal.'[36] But, as is well known, Bradley refused to identify the Absolute with the God of religion; he maintains that 'if you identify the Absolute with God, that is not the God of religion'.[37] Bradley thought that the God of religion must be a finite person having thoughts and feelings like ordinary persons otherwise he would be an inconsistent emptiness. The whole point of my argument in the following chapter will be to establish the contrary. I want to hold that it makes good sense to talk of a God who is personal in an extraordinary sense, a God who is super- or supra-personal.

So far, I have tried to show, firstly the logical affinity between the words 'holy' and 'holiness' on the one hand, and 'God' on the other. Secondly, I have taken the further step of

---

[31] *Essays and Addresses on the Philosophy of Religion* p. 50. (Dent, 1921).
[32] *Philosophical Theology* Vol. II p. 166. (Cambridge, 1930).
[33] *God in Christian Thought and Experience* p. 179. (Nisbet, 1930).
[34] *Our Knowledge of God.* p. 251.
[35] *Philosophical Theology* Vol. II p. 166.
[36] *Appearance and Reality* p. 471. (Clarendon, 1930).
[37] ibid. p. 395.

trying to show the very close logical affinity between the word
'God' and 'person'; indeed they can be used interchangeably
when the latter term has a qualifier such as 'complete', 'perfect', 'supra' or 'super' combined with it. Having arrived at
this stage we are in a position to tackle the problem of showing
what is meant by 'person' when combined with such qualifiers
as those just mentioned, and in view of the close relationship
which I hold to exist between the three terms 'Holy', 'God' and
'person'-plus-qualifier, any light that can be thrown upon the
meaning of the last term should illuminate the first at the same
time.

CHAPTER X

DIVINE PERSONALITY
AND THE PERFECT VISION

I MUST at the outset distinguish between my use of the word
'personality' here and a popular use where we have in mind
chiefly the striking, impressive characteristics of a particular
person. The clumsy word 'personhood' would perhaps be more
suitable for what I want to discuss were it not so cacophonous,
but there is no reason why the word 'personality' should not
serve just as well provided we bear in mind the caveat I have
just made. I want to consider what is essential for a person to
be a person at all.

If an answer to this question can be provided then we should
be in a better position to say something about the problem
precipitated at the end of the last chapter, namely, the problem
of making clear what is meant by 'divine person'. What, then,
do we mean by the word 'person'? This question is a vast one
as it stands, so what I propose to do is to focus attention upon
what seems to me to be a distinctive characteristic of personality. The distinctive characteristic which I have in mind is
intelligence. But then of course we need to explain what is
meant by intelligence, and this is itself another complex question. So I propose to take up what I regard as the distinctive
and essential feature of intelligence and centre my discussion
on that. Intelligence, I shall suggest, is to be understood in
terms of insights and visions of various degrees which people
have in various situations. We can conceive of a vision however
which so far surpasses all others that it stands quite alone and
aloof—this is what I shall call the 'perfect vision'. My claim is
not that any of us can have, or even share, such a vision but
only that we can conceive of there being such a vision. Whoever had such a vision as this would be a person of quite extraordinary intelligence—an exceptional person indeed. Such I
would suggest is the 'divine person' who is the Holy One, who

is himself the paradigm case of holiness and the source of holiness in everything and everyone else. From this bare outline of the view which I now want to discuss in more detail it will be seen that the concept of a perfect vision is the key concept in terms of which the concept of 'divine personality' is to be illuminated, and in view of the close logical kinship between the latter concept and that of holiness one may hope that the concept of 'perfect vision' will eventually help to organize what I have said about holiness in earlier chapters.

To return then to my point about the distinctive characteristic of a person qua person. That a person is pre-eminently an intelligent being is borne out if we consider what we expect of a person, and also how we treat him. In the first place we expect him to be capable of purposive behaviour in some measure. There is no need to draw hard and fast lines here; it is sufficient to say that the more purposive behaviour a being exemplifies, the happier we are about ascribing personality to such a being, and vice versa. It is, of course, a popular practice to speak of certain events in nature, and of the behaviour of certain pieces of machinery, in terms of purpose. Such a use of the word 'purpose' is analogical, but it raises the question: what is distinctive about human purposive behaviour in its primary sense? It seems to me that the most distinctive thing about human purposive behaviour is that it involves having some measure of insight into a more or less complex situation. It involves grasping or seeing interconnections between certain things done and the results that follow, between what we generally call means and ends. We often ask people why they did so and so precisely because we expect them to be able to connect what they did with some desired end; we assume that they possess an insight into the relevant situation, an insight which for some reason or other we would like to share when we ask why.

Admittedly, not all distinctively personal behaviour is purposive. People laugh or cry; they dance with joy or cover their heads in grief. Yet such behaviour as this could hardly be accounted personal unless there was a certain measure of insight into the relevant situation. We expect a person to be able to explain why he laughs or mourns. He must have 'seen' the joke; he must have 'realized' his loss, and so on. Thus a hyaena can make a laughing sound and a crocodile can shed tears, but we do not take their behaviour as personal precisely because we do not consider their 'ha ha's' and tears to follow from any particular intellectual insight or understanding.

Furthermore, we expect a person to be to some degree consistent in his behaviour, but it is important to note that a mechanistic consistency is not enough. In so far as one were consistent through compulsion or conditioning alone, the consistency would not distinctively mark such behaviour as personal. Indeed we might want to say of such a one, in some circumstances, that he was depersonalized. The consistency that we associate with personality is taken as following from certain views which a person holds, and we expect such consistency of behaviour because we assume that a person grasps the implications of his views. It is for a similar reason that we expect a person to be able to argue for his point of view and bring out the reasons for holding it.

Another feature of our treatment of persons, qua persons, is our habit of ascribing responsibility to them, and of praising or blaming them. We normally do this, however, only in so far as we have reason to believe that they 'realize' what they have done and have 'seen' the implications and results of their deeds. Once more, insight—an intelligent understanding of a situation—is of paramount importance in our estimation of a being as personal.

Finally, we expect a person to be one who could be educated, and when we ponder this fact the importance of insight once more emerges. It is not a capacity for accumulating and retaining factual information that distinctively marks a being as personal, but a capacity to correlate them, to grasp theories which explain them, to produce new theories and explanations and so forth. Mere capacity for rote learning and retention of facts is usually downgraded and called 'mechanical', these being just the sort of tasks for which machines can now be produced.

These few very general remarks will have to suffice on this vast question of what personality consists in. What I have done is to pick on one factor which seems to me to be of central importance. In the absence of this factor in a particular case purposive action and the capacity to give reasons for action completely disappear, any consistency of behaviour and memory feats will be regarded as mechanical, and we shall be disinclined to ascribe responsibility to the being in question. That is, we could not regard such a being as a person. Wherever and whenever this all-important factor is present however, the situation becomes personal. Think of a situation in which one sees a few scattered, apparently unrelated, items which have aroused our interest, and consider how our attitude in that situation changes when we begin to relate the items, when a plan emerges, and we eventually realize that a person must have been at work. It then becomes appropriate to ask: who is responsible? why did he do this? and so forth. Situations can, no doubt, become personal in many different ways but I would suggest that they never do so unless and until we are convinced that they bespeak intelligent insight to some degree. Now since God, the Holy One, is regarded by his worshippers as a person, we may ask if he is an intelligent being, and whether his intelligence also is to be understood in terms of insight or vision. He is, of course, an extraordinary 'person', a divine 'person', so we should expect that if he is to be understood at all in terms of intelligence and insight or vision, then the intelligence and vision in question would be extraordinary indeed.

There can be no doubt that it has been generally maintained by theists that God is an intelligent being. F. R. Tennant held that, whatever else the divine nature may or may not include, 'it is at least characterized by intelligence'.[1] Certainly no theist would want to say that God is unintelligent, though some might want to maintain that God is altogether beyond the intelligent/unintelligent distinction. We could take a middle course and commend the attribution of intelligence to God only with the proviso that a qualifier such as 'divine' or 'perfect' is combined with it to show that God's intelligence is not on a level with human intelligence. This I believe to be the best procedure and part of my task will be to consider what intelligence in the qualified sense could mean, but I can also imagine that some theists would prefer to reject the term 'intelligence'

[1] *Philosophical Theology* Vol. II p. 166.

altogether, and there is at least one reason for doing this which deserves consideration.

Professor Ryle holds, in his book *Concept of Mind*, that 'it is of the essence of intelligent practices that one performance is modified by its predecessors. The agent is still learning.'[2] It seems that on this view, a person who is not in a position to improve himself or who is not in the position of a learner, cannot be intelligent, and since it is generally maintained that God is in no sense a learner there would seem to be good reason for saying that the word 'intelligence' is not at all applicable in his case. But Ryle's statement is questionable. It is sufficient reason for calling a practice 'intelligent' if (a) there are good reasons for continuing the practice in its present form and (b) certain dispositional conditions are fulfilled, such as readiness to modify appropriately or abandon the practice in the face of certain alterations in the circumstances. Provided these conditions hold, a practice may be habitual but also intelligent at the same time. Some habits are admittedly stupid, but are there not a few intelligent ones as well? Improvement in behaviour and practice is a very good sign of, but not a *sine qua non* of, intelligence. Thus the fact that a person is intelligent does not entail that he is a learner, and the reason suggested above for denying that intelligence can be attributed to God is disposed of.

Very near kinsmen of the word 'intelligent' are 'rational' and 'logical', and these are the terms which Professor L. Hodgson uses in his *Towards a Christian Philosophy*. He maintains that the divine personal life 'is the one reality which is perfect in its logical self-consistency', and that the will of God 'is the source of all the reason and logic in creation'.[3] We may take it then that some eminent theists at any rate believe that God is intelligent, rational, logical, self-consistent, and my quotation from Hodgson's book exemplifies the use of the qualifying term 'perfect' of which we must always take good note. Hodgson is using the word 'logical' in a loose sense which present-day logicians would hardly recommend. The words 'logical inconsistency' would usually be taken to refer to the case where

---

[2] *Concept of Mind* p. 42. (Hutchinson, 1949).
[3] *Towards a Christian Philosophy* p. 150. (Nisbet, 1942).

what is said involves or implies a proposition of the form '*p* and not *p*'. Logical consistency or inconsistency applies pre-eminently to statements, not to things or reality.

Hodgson is not using the word 'logic' in this strict, tight sense, for he refers to God as a 'logical and self-consistent reality' and also suggests that reason and logic are to be found in the creation. Logic, for him, 'is in things before it is in human thought'.[4] We have really two contentions here, one about the self-consistency of God and the other about the consistency of things and I now want to consider the latter at some length. On the face of it, it would seem that *things* cannot be consistent or inconsistent, logical or illogical, and that to talk as if they could looks like what Professor Ryle would call a category mistake. But I still think that Hodgson has a point which I eventually hope to bring out more clearly.

I take the liberty of taking 'things' to mean 'states of affairs'. It must be admitted that things are always seen from some point of view or other; they are seen in the light of some sort of understanding, in the light of someone's experience, or in the light of what we might call his way of looking at things. In the case of the scientist they may be seen in the light of a theory. Now, it does make sense to assert that things are inconsistent if the claim is prefaced by such words as 'in the light of. . . .' where the blank is filled by words like 'my experience', 'my way of looking at things', 'this theory'. To take an example where things are seen in the light of a theory. Newton could sensibly say that in the light of his gravitational theory a state of affairs in which a stone remains stationary in mid-air with no detectable support would be inconsistent. The reason why there would be sense in Newton's contention here is not far to seek. His gravitational theory is statable in fairly precise terms, and so would be the description of the state of affairs where the stone stood in mid-air, and if the two stories were integrated then a proposition of the form '*p* and not *p*' would be made somewhere, or else implied in what was said. The inconsistency turns out in the last analysis to be a logical one in the strict sense.

Take another example, where I preface my story by 'in the

4 *Towards a Christian Philosophy* p. 29.

light of my experience' and go on to say that the state of affairs in which a river goes under a bridge in the direction north to south on one side, but in the opposite direction on the other, is inconsistent. Here again statements which are inconsistent would be involved in the integrating of the two stories; in the light of my experience I should say 'every river goes in the same direction on both sides of a bridge', but the description of the posited state of affairs in our example would include a statement to the effect that one river goes in opposite directions on the two sides of the bridge. Along these lines one might contend that things can be inconsistent and illogical, or otherwise. If a philosophically unsophisticated person says of a certain state of affairs 'it is inconsistent', he may well have a meaningful point to make, and fortunately the point is usually understood independently of the philosopher's analysis. The real point can always be saved by adding such provisoes as I have suggested.

The point 'can be saved' I say, but it could be lost too if the provisoes are not produced. Unless this is done it is open to someone else to emphasize the opposite point by making a different proviso, by adding 'in themselves', for instance, to 'things'. Things in themselves independently of our view, of our way of looking at them, of our theories, are not consistent or inconsistent, logical or illogical. Of course, our theories are not everything we could wish them to be. On the flat-earth view it would be an inconsistent, an impossible, state of affairs for a person to travel along the surface of the earth in the same direction and eventually arrive at his starting point. It is obvious today that such states of affairs do not involve any inconsistency; it was only in the light of the flat-earth view that they would seem inconsistent. When things that seem inconsistent, and therefore quite impossible in the light of certain theories, do in fact happen then there is nothing for it but to modify or change those theories. States of affairs precede theories and points of view, and that is why there is so much point in saying that in themselves, independently of our point of view and of our theories, things are not consistent or inconsistent; they just are.

Yet it is possible to take this point too far, for things are nearly always seen from some point of view or other, in the light of somebody's experience, or in the light of some theory or other. The nearest we can imagine to an impartial observer would be a new-born child whose first experiences would be quite unprecedented. No background of experience or point of view would be involved here, but the baby would also be the last of all to raise questions about consistency and inconsistency of the universe! To him, if to anyone, things just are, but to people who have reached an age and maturity when they discuss things, make claims to know certain things and so on, everything is seen and appreciated in the light of some background of experience, and is therefore seen as involving consistency or inconsistency. Further, since in fact we do not see anything except as involving consistency or inconsistency, it is only a small step from this to saying that everything is consistent or inconsistent, and that is quite permissible so long as we understand the nature of our claim. We show that we do understand the nature of this claim by our readiness to relate consistency or inconsistency to a definite expressible point of view, background or theory.

This is a convenient place for calling back the terms 'intelligent' and 'reason' which have been shelved while I discussed logic and the idea of consistency. Roughly speaking, we should say that, in so far as a person has a point of view which enables him to give an explanation of the facts of the world around him, that person is intelligent. This point of view may just as well be manifest in his general behaviour or his way of doing a particular job as in anything he says. It involves what at a lower level we call 'understanding' and at a higher level 'insight', the difference being that the object of understanding is usually something which somebody else has already perceived and which is in process of being clarified to us, whereas a person is said to have an insight when he himself gets hold of something that is quite new. The second would be considered a higher instance of intelligence than the first. Reasoning is involved when we justify a certain point of view or theory, or try to explain its implications. An intelligent person would be expected to reason well, and to reason well is to reason logically and consistently. Perhaps one could say that reason is in creation but only in a derivative sense; what I said of logic and consistency as existing in the world, in things, or in states of affairs, holds for reason too.

Having said this much by way of explaining how the terms 'intelligent', 'logic' and 'reason' join hands, I should now like to concentrate attention upon what I referred to as insight, for it seems to me that this brings us to the crux of the matter. I have already used some very vague terms—'point of view', 'way of looking at things', and 'theory'. Whatever one may have in mind when using such phrases or words there is generally a reference, close or remote, to some kind of insight by which the point of view and so on, are acquired. Some insights issue in a better understanding of intricate logical points, some in theories, some in new interpretations of human behaviour and of history.

Another name that might be given to these insights is 'visions', but the kind of vision I have in mind at the moment is to be distinguished sharply from such experiences as those to which mystics have applied this name. It is not anything like the experience of the person who has a 'vision' of Gabriel or the Virgin Mary that is intended by the word as I want to use it now, but something far more like what F. Waismann means by it when he explains his view of philosophy in his contribution to the book *Contemporary British Philosophy* and maintains that the most essential feature of philosophy is 'vision'.[5] Waismann, referring to the discoveries of Descartes, Einstein and Hilbert, emphasizes how wrong it is to think of them as the result of a method or procedure, 'as if the great men arrived a their solutions by drawing logical inferences'.[6] He points out that 'this leaves out the most essential thing—the flashing of a new aspect which is *non*-inferential'.[6] The visions which Waismann discusses issue in fundamental changes of outlook, though he does also give examples of what he calls 'more or less trivial cases'.[6]

These insights could be seen as forming a scale extending from the trivial or minor insights into a particular situation at one end, to vastly more far-reaching visions at the other. An example of a minor insight would be the solving of a Binet in-

[5] *Contemporary British Philosophy* p. 483. (Allen & Unwin, 1956).
[6] ibid. p. 488.

telligence test, while the most revolutionary scientific discoveries constitute examples of vision nearer the other end of the scale. Mention of intelligence tests reminds us that an accepted criterion of intelligence is behaviour which manifests insights. The deeper the insights gained the greater the intelligence involved; we should generally agree to name Newton or Einstein as examples of people who were highly intelligent. It is also worthy of note that just as insight bespeaks intelligence in the person who has it, so also does it impart intelligibility to what is seen. We can say of insights and visions that they render situations, facts, things or states of affairs, *intelligible.*

Reason comes into the scene when we start working out the implications of our insights. If we succeed in our argument, our view will be commended as reasonable, and if the insight is a far-reaching one with wide implications there are some who will say that in its light things—the universe and so on—make sense. Some will proclaim that it shows how much reason there is in the universe, but more of this later. Reason involves consistency, and the test of consistency is certainly a crucial one for any theory, metaphysic, or Weltanschauung, which is the product of insight or vision. Such a criterion will be applied in different ways according as to whether the insight is expressed in a scientific theory on the one hand, or a myth or parable on the other. In the latter case the seeker of consistency will have to go very carefully, but the exponent of the myth or parable has a comparable responsibility in seeking a meeting-point with such a seeker; to avoid such a meeting-point is to escape judgement at the expense of losing respect. Even the myth must engage at some point or other with ordinary language.

It is possible, in the light of what I have already said about visions, not only to have a scale of visions, but also to have visions within visions. Thus it will be possible for two people to argue against each other for or against a view on a particular issue in the light of a wider outlook which both hold in common. Two Thomists, two Idealists, or two Positivists might well argue against each other on particular points while agreeing in each case in their basic outlook. Similarly, there may be more than one way of interpreting a scientific theory with regard to particular instances so that we could have two exponents of the same theory arguing against each other on a particular issue. Argument at this level is very much a matter of hammering out internal inconsistencies and working out the logic of a position. Whenever two people hold opposed views on some point or other rational argument between them is possible so long as there is a wider viewpoint which both share, and which supplies common premises from which argument can proceed. Of course we sometimes find ourselves assuming a common viewpoint only to discover that our opponent disagrees with us at a more fundamental level. In that case we have to fall back upon a still more fundamental shared viewpoint and proceed from there.

To return now to our scale of visions, as we get towards the end of the scale where visions have very far-reaching implications there is less and less room for argument between those who accept and those who reject the view. When we come to the deepest insights of all, it is practically impossible to argue with a person who does not share them with us. There are no common premises from which the arguments may proceed, and it is then a matter of changing a whole intellectual outlook. People are not argued into such viewpoints; they are converted to them. The best the protagonist of a basically new attitude can do is to explain it to his fellowman, to try to get the latter to understand it. Conversion may come with the initial understanding or at a later date when the fuller implications are realized.

I have tried to show how intelligence implies an insight or vision, and that these insights or visions can be thought of as being at some point or other on a scale. I have also suggested that a vision's place on the scale could be decided according to whether its acceptance called for rational vindication or conversion. The insights that belong to the conversion end of the scale might fittingly be called 'higher' than the others, and as I have suggested above, the person who has such visions or insights could be called *highly* intelligent. Indeed, we do sometimes speak of an intellect of the stature of Einstein for instance as being super-intelligent. We are at last in a position to consider what can be meant by 'perfect intelligence', or by what Hodgson called 'the source of all the reason and logic in creation',[7] and I want to suggest that these words can best be understood in terms of a 'perfect vision'.

THE PERFECT VISION

I want to suggest that there can be a vision which is very different indeed from any that we already possess. It would be the perfect vision, quite beyond even the highest that we can conceive of. In its light everything, every state of affairs, all facts, would be perfectly intelligible; no inconsistency could arise within it for the working out of its implications would be perfectly logical.

So big is the jump from the visions that I have discussed so far to the one mentioned in this last paragraph that we need again to face the question which someone is sure to raise: but what does the word 'vision' mean now? And with this should come a quest also for the meaning of 'logic' and 'reason' in the new context. Examples were produced of insights and visions in the first part of my discussion, but we have no examples of the perfect vision. So what are we to make of the latter? We can do two things here, firstly, we can look back and realize what the step has been like when men of great insight have broken through to a new vision of things in the past, and secondly we can look forward and imagine the possibility of a new vision of things in the future which will change our outlook in a radical way again. We have no inkling of what such an insight could be, or how things would look in the light of it, nor again what its rational implications would be, and how it would alter our ways of reasoning. But we can imagine the possibility of such an insight or vision. Furthermore, we can imagine this first future vision being surpassed by a second, and the second by a third, and so on, until we come to what I have called the perfect vision. The term 'perfect vision' is meaningful if it is thought of as labelling a member of such a series as I have described. Being a *perfect* vision, it could not itself ever be surpassed by another and, since every member in the posited

---

[7] *Towards a Christian Philosophy* p. 150.

series could be improved upon except the last, the perfect vision itself would have to be the last one of the series. Incidentally, I do not wish to suggest that an ordinary human person could ever be converted to the viewpoint of this perfect vision. He is incapable of having it, otherwise he would be God; he can only worship the extraordinary, divine person who has the perfect vision.

Someone might now ask: but why should there be a last member of the series at all? why shouldn't the series of visions keep on progressing indefinitely? This question can only be answered by saying something further about the nature of the series, of which the perfect vision is the final term. There are two types of series which might be distinguished as follows. One seems to be by its very nature endless, while the other naturally leads to a final term. Stringing words together, or piling bricks, would be an example of the first type, and it is a task that could, in principle, go on for ever. The series that leads to the perfect vision is *not* of this kind. As an example of the second type consider the series of insights by which a poet produces a poem. The poet proceeds by little, or greater, leaps of insight which gives him a line here, a new word there, a new idea for a stanza or verse, or even a new framework for the whole poem. Sooner or later the poet arrives at a point of relative satisfaction; at least he is willing for the poem to be published under his name. This point would be reached when the poet felt that any further change would detract from, rather than enhance, the quality of his work. The work itself convinces him that there is no room for a further helpful insight. It is of course debatable whether any poet is finally justified in coming to such a conclusion, and it is a well-known fact that the best artists are often dissatisfied with their work even when they present it as their complete product. R. G. Collingwood, in his book *An Autobiography*, goes as far as to say that 'no "work of art" is ever finished, so that in that sense of the phrase there is no such thing as a "work of art" at all. Work ceases upon the picture or manuscript, not because it is finished, but because sending-in day is at hand, or because the printer is clamorous for copy, or because "I am sick of working at this thing" or "I can't see what more I can do to it" '.[8] One would hesitate before affirming that any particular poem is perfect, but it is not inconceivable that a poem should be perfect. It seems to me that it is of the nature of any art that it aims at completion and perfection. The conclusion of such a work has what Dr Austin Farrer has called 'poetical inevitability'.[9]

Again, consider the differences between piling up bricks and building a church; one could go on piling up bricks for ever without anything in the nature of the work itself calling for a stop, but we could not go on building a church for ever without the church eventually ceasing to be a church at all. The church might indeed be on such a vast scale that there would seem to be no hope of completing it within the span of human life on our planet, but the building of such a church as this even would be in principle, and essentially, a job that could be completed. Similarly, a poem is essentially a thing that can be completed. If one just went on and on bringing in one thing after another into the work without aiming at, or intending, any kind of completion whatever then that work simply would not be a poem. One could of course, in principle, compose on a vast scale and include in our work a reference to everything in the whole universe, but the requirement that the work should come to an end somewhere still holds if the work is to be called a poem.

The important thing to realize here is that the series of moves involved in building a church or writing a poem is not brought to an end by a shortage of material, bricks or words. It is brought to an end by the inherent completeness of a personal vision of the architect or poet. When the vision has been fully expressed there is no need for any more bricks or words. This completion is therefore not a limit set upon the vision from the outside as would be the case where one could not pile up any more bricks because there were no more bricks available. The completion is due to the completeness of the vision itself.

The perfect vision I take to be an end term in a series of this latter kind; it is a series which is essentially terminable. It seems to me that this way of understanding the perfect vision

---

[8] *An Autobiography* p. 2. (Oxford, 1939).
[9] *The Glass of Vision* p. 139. (Dacre Press, 1949).

does justice to the theistic contentions that the universe is purposive and that it is a creation. These are precisely the contentions that we should make about poems and churches. Stringing words together or piling up bricks are, as such, mechanical operations, non-purposive and non-creative, while a poem or a beautiful church is the expression of purposive activity and is a creative production. In both religious and artistic fields the product of a vision is purposive and creative, and it is therefore not unreasonable to hold that there is something similar in the nature of the completion involved in both cases.

Yet, though the perfect vision is like poetic vision in this way, the former is quite superior to the latter in the following way. A poem which perfectly expresses the poet's vision could not receive any additional material without being marred. Even a single word added to a poem that is worthy of being called a classic would detract from its perfect completeness, much more so if an extra sentence or verse were added. Such additional matter would either be already better expressed in the poem or else it would be outside the subject-matter of the particular poem in question. But the fact that there could be such additional subject-matter at all shows that the poem, though perfect in its own way and as an expression of one particular vision, is still finite in relation to the whole of life and the universe. There can be other poems.[10] The perfect vision differs from a particular poetic vision in that there is no other insight that can mar it. In the light of the perfect vision it is not that nothing more could be said on this or that particular subject but that nothing more could be said about anything at all. The universe is perfectly explicable in its light, and it is therefore without limit and infinite.

If there was indeed such a perfect vision then all the insights and visions that men have had, and do have, could be seen as cases of understanding what has, for perfect intelligence, always been in view. I have maintained above that we can only have logic and reason within the span of some viewpoint or other, and that there is a possibility of talking about logic and reason in creation only in so far as it is considered from some

---

[10] Speaking of works of art, Collingwood says: 'the number of such works is therefore of necessity infinite'. *Speculum Mentis* p. 70-71. (Clarendon, 1924).

viewpoint or other. If, as I now suggest, we can talk of a perfect viewpoint which is prior to all others, then there is sense in claiming that there is logic and reason in creation even apart from any particular viewpoint that we at any stage happen to possess. And this, it seems to me, is the important point which is preserved in Hodgson's contention that ' "logic" is in things before it is in human thought'.[11] When he further refers to God as being the 'source of all the reason and logic in creation' then I should interpret this as being a reference to perfect intelligence. These words should not therefore be dismissed as being an instance of a category mistake, for they can be seen as making a significant claim. If the claim that there is logic in things is taken as implying that they can be seen in the light of a perfect vision, then the claim that logic is in things *before* it is in human thought implies that there is a vision which is distinct from any human one. The extraordinary character of this vision can be brought out by a consideration of Dr Hodgson's further contention that God is the 'source of all the reason and logic in creation'. Since it is only when things are seen in the light of a certain vision that we can sensibly say that there is logic in things, it is not misleading to say that the vision is the source of that logic. Then the vision which could be described as the 'source of all the logic and reason in creation' would be that which I have hitherto called the perfect vision, and we can now understand Dr Hodgson's words as a contention that God has this perfect vision.

We are not ourselves in possession of the perfect vision, and therefore we do not know what the logic and reason which is implied in the vision is like. We do not know what is the nature of this 'logic and reason which is in creation'. Reason and logic have a vast arbitrariness about them. We are well aware of the great difference between modern symbolic logic and Aristotelian logic though the former does not set out to contradict the latter at each point but incorporates its valid points in a more comprehensive system. But who knows that a particular scheme of symbolic logic will not be transcended by as great a degree as that by which it transcended Aristotelian logic? The perfect vision would indeed incorporate and extend beyond all finite

[11] *Towards a Christian Philosophy* p. 29.

rational patterns, and I have suggested above that the universe is a creative expression of that perfect vision—a vision which is there independently of our finite understanding of it. It seems to me that we can appreciate Hodgson's contention that there is logic in things before it is in human thought as emphasizing precisely this point.

Now we begin to see how valuable and illuminating this concept of a 'perfect vision' can be. Hodgson's words provide us with a good example of a traditional discussion of God—the sort of discussion however which some present-day critics would regard as obscure if not meaningless. But once this concept of a 'perfect vision' is brought into the context we can begin to appreciate the sense and force of Hodgson's remarks. It is in such a way as this, I would hope, that the concept of a 'perfect vision' can throw still more light on the use and meaning of the words 'God', 'the Holy One' and 'holiness'.

There are two possible objections that might be raised at this point, one by the theist and the other by the agnostic philosopher. I shall take the theist's objection first. He might feel that by interpreting divine intelligence in terms of a perfect vision which is the last in a finite series we are doing away with the infinity which theists have always claimed for God. In answer to this I should first point out that, from the fact that the perfect vision is the last in a finite series, it by no means follows that this final vision is itself finite. It is quite the contrary. Finitude implies limits and limits can only fall *within* a vision. We cannot speak of the limits of a vision in terms of the vision itself. No theory can be its own critic. But of course we can show up a particular vision as limited in range by bringing it into the light of another vision which extends beyond it. Thus a vision x can be shown to be limited only if we have a wider vision y from which to look at x and see beyond it. I have contended that the perfect vision is such that it cannot be superseded. Thus, if the perfect vision be x, then there cannot possibly be another vision y from which x could be seen as limited. So x cannot be limited or finite, and should therefore be called infinite. My account, far from endangering a fundamental theistic tenet, confirms it.

I come now to the second objection, the discussion of which

will take us much further afield. The sceptical philosopher might agree that the term 'perfect vision' could have the sort of logical placing which I suggest; he might agree that it makes some sense to talk of a 'perfect vision'. But he would then perhaps want to round this off with an explanation in dispositional terms. He would show how the perfect vision could be described as that which human beings may have or could have one day in the future. Let us say that a person P has had a vision *a* at a certain stage in his life, that this vision was superseded by vision *b* and that at the present time he may be seeing things in the light of vision *c*. Surely, it makes sense to say that he might have a vision that is beyond these, which we could call *n*. We do not as yet know what *n* is, for it is only a possibility. So also we might say that P or some other person in the remote future perhaps could have a vision which was perfect. On this view there is no need to suppose that anyone actually has the perfect vision now, still less that something is being accomplished in the light of a perfect vision.

If we do want to maintain that there actually is a person who has this vision then, so our opponent would maintain, we have much further to travel. In all this I would agree with the opponent, and I believe that the theist must face up to the challenge and show that by 'God' he means more than a future human being who will see things in the light of a perfect vision; 'God' is not simply a name for the ultimate perfection which is in process of being realized in human intellectual progress. So now I must try to put more substance in my claim, and it seems to me that this can best be done by referring to the Christian doctrine of creation *ex nihilo*. Let us consider what is meant when we speak of the creative activity of God.

I shall begin by considering what we mean by creation in nontheistic language. To take an example, we should say that a great painter is engaged in creative work when he is painting a picture. In trying to find out what is the nature of the claim when it is asserted that such a work is creative it is helpful to make clear in the first place what is not creative, so let us do this with reference to our example. When we are searching for the creative element in the painter's task it is not entirely beside the point to notice the colours he uses, but if it is the pigment as pigment, or the colour as being absorption and reflection of certain light rays, that engages our attention then we are missing the point. The painter's way of handling his brush is also relevant to his creative activity, but to concentrate attention entirely upon the physical mechanics of the muscular movements of his hand and arm is again to miss the point. It may be possible to show that the painter's arm would not move as it does unless there were certain physical changes of some kind in the brain, so that we should have to agree that these changes are involved in the artist's creative work too. But once more we are, in seeking what is meant by calling the artist's work 'creative', going up the wrong lane if we become completely engrossed in a study of the physiology of the human brain.

We could be in full possession of a very comprehensive scientific account of the nature of colours, of muscular movement, and of brain-cell changes, and yet be none the wiser as to what is meant by calling the painter's total activity creative. We might be presented with two equally comprehensive accounts covering all that took place while two different people, one a great painter, the other a novice, painted a canvas and yet be utterly at a loss as to which of the performances was creative and which not. What then are we claiming when we say that a certain artist creates?

Consider another example where a friend draws a very good accurate picture of a familiar object, but depicts it as seen from a very unfamiliar angle. Every now and then as he proceeds with the drawing he stops to ask: 'Do you see what it's going to be?' The answer is always 'no'. He finally completes the picture and we are still puzzled as to what it is supposed to represent. We have seen the object often enough but have never taken any notice of what it looks like from this particular angle, and so we remain baffled. When, and if, we do find out what the picture represents the discovery comes all of a sudden; then we will see what we have been staring at the whole time in a very different way. This might not inappropriately be called a case of having a new vision, of 'seeing' something new though we had already seen everything before in one sense of 'seeing'.

The second sense of the word 'see' which my last example was intended to bring out provides a clue to the way we are to appreciate the creative aspect of the artist's activity.[12] The essence of creation is vision which finds expression in the artist's work, a vision which the beholder must also share if he is to appreciate the claim that this artist is creative. The vision involved in my example of a friend and the object drawn from an unusual angle was a trivial one, and we should hardly claim that the friend was creative. The creative artist must go further than this, otherwise he will merely receive the rather dubious compliment of being called 'clever'. He will only be called creative if he has a vision more or less penetrating, and succeeds in expressing that vision in his picture, or pictures. It may be a vision of the values and effect of colours and the way they affect each other in juxtaposition, or into shapes and the way they can be arranged so as to give an illusion of space and so forth. The vision is such that it cannot be expressed except in the work of art itself. Thus, if we want to draw attention to the creative power of an artist we do not give a physicist's account of what happened as he painted, but point to the picture itself and give our friend whatever aid we can by way of leading him to an appreciative vision of the work in question. This account of human creativity could be extended to include examples from the realm of the poet, the dramatist, the musician, and from any other field of creative activity.

Although the vision of which we speak is not a physical cause or a link in any scientific description of what happens when an artist paints, yet its importance must not be underestimated. It is still true that the picture would not be there, or would not be what it is, except for the vision. Thus, even though we may imagine the scientific description to be as complete as we like, something of radical importance would be missing from our account of the whole situation unless we brought in a reference to the artist's vision. The artist's vision is not a member, not even the first member, in the sequence of physical changes which take place when the artist performs his task, yet the vision is in some sense the basis of the whole sequence. It would also be an oversimplification if the word

[12] cf. p. 21.

'vision' were explained away in terms of the finished product to such an extent that the word was equated in meaning with 'this picture' uttered in the appropriate situation. This would involve either reducing the word 'vision' to refer to a physical object or elevating the words 'this picture' to such a level that we should have to say, very clumsily, that this paint-on-canvas would not be what it is except for this picture. I maintain that the artist's vision does 'account for' his picture's being what it is although it is not the physical cause of the picture, and this 'accounting for' is creation.

It is obvious by now how my account of divine creativity is going to run. The universe is the product of divine creation, but it is important to understand what is the nature of this claim. It is possible to have a very comprehensive scientific under-standing of the nature of the physical universe and yet fail to see it as a creation. There is a way of looking at the universe, of employing our senses to the full and exercising our brain to its utmost capacity, which nevertheless does not take us one step nearer to seeing the universe as a creation.

Divine creativity may be understood best by referring back to the perfect vision which was discussed earlier. The universe is the expression of the perfect vision, and to appreciate fully the nature of divine creation it would be necessary for us to have that vision ourselves. Although no human being can claim to have this perfect vision, yet we can still sensibly say that the universe is the expression of a perfect vision just as one could sensibly maintain that a picture was the result of a great creative power in the artist even though we might not be in a position to appreciate that creative power and could not ourselves see *how* the picture was really a creative product. It is something to claim *that* the universe is the expression of a vision even when we are very far from knowing *what* the vision is like.

Since the word 'universe' is so imprecise one could profitably recast the argument of the last paragraph in the following form. Scientific visions or insights enable us to see certain aspects of the world as intelligible patterns. The structure of the atom will serve as an example. When the scientist perceives this pattern he is not only engaged in imaginative and creative work, though that comes into it to a greater degree than is often realized, but also in something which still deserves to be called 'discovery'. There is a sense in which we can say that the atom would be there whether the scientist understood it or not. The atom does not depend upon the scientist's insight in the *same* way as a picture depends upon the painter's vision. In the latter case the picture would not be anything like what it is except for the artist's vision. The theist's claim can be understood as implying that the pattern which the scientist discovers would not exist except for the perfect vision of God. Just as a picture may be said to originate in a vision so the atom, for instance, originates in the perfect vision and would not be what it is except for that perfect vision. Again, it must be emphasized that this vision is not a physical constituent which accounts for the formation of the atom; to suppose this would be to slip into the same error as does the person who thinks he can understand what the creative power of the artist is by examining the muscular contractions of his arms.

The theist may, once again, raise an objection to my argument. He will remind me that divine creation is *ex nihilo*, and that in this respect it differs fundamentally from the artist's creation. This difference is quite rightly emphasized, and indeed I need only draw out some of the implications of my argument to show more clearly the force of this *ex nihilo* claim.

Let us make clear the difference between what we might call the artist's creation and the pre-existent material which he used in his creative work. The artist's creative product on the one hand is that which derives from a vision, that is, it is precisely that which could not have existed but for the artist's vision. It is the picture as 'seen' in the light of a certain appreciative vision. The pre-existing material, on the other hand, is just that which would still exist if the artist never had a vision. This material consists, in the artist's case, of pigment, canvas and so forth, and the artist's vision has nothing at all to do with these as materials having certain chemical constitutions. In this respect they are independent of the artist's vision and are preexistent in relation to the artist's creative work.

The perfect vision, which is our chief concern here, differs from the artist's in that it is not limited in any way. There is no scientific vision of the structure of the universe which is not included in the perfect vision. The theist may say that the table in my room would not be what it is but for the perfect vision; the wonderful cell-pattern which comprises it would not exist as *this* pattern unless there was a perfect vision any more than the artist's picture would exist without his vision. But, granted that a vision accounts for the cells being formed in a certain pattern, are not the cells pre-existent material in this case? The theist may answer that they are composed of a pattern of molecules, and that *this* pattern would not exist but for the perfect comprehensive divine vision. If the molecules themselves are now held up as candidates for the title 'pre-existent material', the theist can still point out that they are themselves a pattern of atomic structures which would not exist but for the perfect vision. Atoms could similarly be claimed as being the result of the perfect vision, and not only atoms, but any possible scientific presentation of any pattern whatever, could be held by the theist to be due to the perfect vision. On this view there could be nothing of which one might say that it existed independently of the perfect vision. There is no candidate for the rôle of pre-existent material in relation to the perfect vision, and that is why it is so appropriate to call that which is attributed to this perfect vision creation *ex nihilo*.

This account of divine creativity marks some advance upon the bare contention that there could be a perfect vision of the universe. There is now just a little more body as it were to the theistic claim. On this view the world is not simply an object for contemplation, but is a creation; for it is not the object, but the expression, of a perfect vision. In so far as this view is acceptable, a certain attitude of concern will be appropriate which would not be appropriate otherwise. The case of the artist and his creation will again serve as an analogy, though a weak one, to bring out my point. Consider the different sorts of interest one might show in the work of the artist. Firstly, one could show a scientific interest in the chemistry of his pigments, or perhaps in the effects on sensation of his juxtaposition of colours. Secondly, one could show an interest in the subjective impressions which the work makes on us, and our reactions towards it. If, however, we view the artist's work as the expression of a creative vision, then we will show a third kind of interest in it, that is, an interest in the intentions of the artist. The picture will be taken as the focal point of a rapport between us and the artist himself.

Somewhat similarly, we can show these three kinds of interest in the world about us and in the general situation in which we find ourselves. There is firstly the scientific interest, and secondly the interest people show by their own experiences of joy, sorrow and so forth, but if we take our situation as being an expression, partial perhaps, of a perfect vision then we shall show another interest in it as well. We shall take it as being intentionally laden and as being a situation in which we can enter into some kind of rapport or relationship with the 'person' whom it bespeaks. Of course this case differs greatly from that of the artist and his work in many respects. The artist expresses himself in something which is relatively static, whereas our world is a living process. Again, we do not ourselves play a part in the artist's finished work, whereas we do figure in the world which expresses the divine vision. Furthermore, in so far as we consider ourselves to be free, our relationship with the 'person' whom the creation bespeaks becomes still more complicated. The divine creation must be infinitely more complex than anything produced by a human artist, and is therefore infinitely more difficult for us to grasp and comprehend.

We should expect a person who showed this kind of interest in his environment and who regards the world as the expression of a perfect creative vision along the lines I have suggested to show a very special kind of concern about his own predicament and his own behaviour in that predicament. From his point of view life and existence will be a matter of playing one's part harmoniously in the creation, and any deviation will constitute a threat to his very existence. Thus for such a person there will be a right and wrong which is more than ordinary moral right and wrong. There will be the right path which fits in with the divine creative vision and the wrong path which does not fit in, which 'cuts one off' and which 'separates' one from it. Since, on the above account, the creative vision is the ground of all existence these paths will be respectively the path of life and that of death, that of existence and that of extinction. Whoever understands his predicament in such a light will want to walk the path of life and whenever he fails he will dread the consequences. Since the perfect vision is by no means within his grasp and is very much a mystery to him he will be very uncertain of his predicament and he will experience an uneasy tension. It will be as though he were striving to get to terms with a mysterious 'person' on whom his very existence depends. In so far as this 'person' is mysterious it will be difficult to know what is pleasing and what is offensive for him, but the tendency will be perhaps for one to go by the dictates of one's conscience, thus one's moral convictions and moral success or failure take on a specially profound significance.

In other words we should expect the man who regards his world as the expression of a perfect creative vision to exhibit just that sort of concern which Hebrew and Christian believers have shown with regard to holiness. For a person who sees his predicament in this light, theistic language, and especially that part of it which centres on the concept of holiness, will have an irresistible attraction. Here he will find a suitable currency for his purpose; he will find the terms in which his interest is discussible. It is for him, more than anyone, that much of what has been said already about holiness will be especially significant.

We can now see why he should find himself talking of God in much the same way as Hebrew and Christian believers have done. We can just about begin to see what sense the word 'God' will have for him. We can turn back to Hebrew and Christian literature and see why it should have been strongly insisted that God is a person and yet equally strongly denied that he is an ordinary person. I have already suggested that where one is confronted with signs of intelligence, that is, with something that can be taken as the expression of a vision, then the situation becomes personal. I would suggest that Hebrew and Christian believers have been convinced that they were confronted with signs of intelligence, and that their situation could be taken as the expression of a vision. If so we can see why they thought of their situation in the world as being a 'personal' one, but the intelligence and the vision expressed was not a human one which human beings could easily grasp, and indeed it was thought to be a mystery from the human point of view. Therefore the personal situation was an extraordinary one, and the person an extraordinary 'person'.

Anyone who regards his world as the expression of a perfect creative vision will also sympathize with Hebrew and Christian conceptions of their relationship with the Holy One. He will be able to make some sense of their fear of, and profound respect for, the holy, and he will be in a position to appreciate how such fear and respect differ from ordinary cases. Again, talk in terms of a mysterious 'power' behind the living universe and of a personal 'power' at work in human history will be meaningful for the person who regards his environmental and historical context in the way I have indicated. From the same viewpoint, one should be able to make some sense of the concept of a personal 'whole' such as I have already discussed, and to grasp what separation from such a 'whole' involves. Finally, the notion of a special standard of holy goodness should now become clearer. What we have here are aspects of the believer's relationship with, and attitude towards, the extraordinary person called God. Now that we have tried to make clearer what is meant by such an extraordinary 'person' in terms of a perfect creative vision, this latter key-concept should help us to see more clearly what is involved in the different aspects of human relationship with such a 'person'. Thus I proceed in my concluding chapter, to reconsider, in the light of our key-concept, each of the points just mentioned above.

CHAPTER XI

CONCLUSION

IN earlier chapters we have seen that the concept of 'holiness' is very closely associated indeed with the concept of 'personality' understood in an exceptional sense, that is, with 'divine personality' and 'God'. This concept of 'divine personality', I have suggested, can best be understood in terms of a 'perfect vision', and we have already seen that this latter concept could help us to understand what religious thinkers have meant by contending that God is the source of all the logic and reason in creation[1] for instance, and again what they have meant by saying that God created the world.[2] This is encouraging, so let us see if this concept of 'perfect vision' can also help to organize and clarify what I have already said about holiness in terms of fear, power, wholeness, separatedness and moral goodness.

It must be admitted that superstitious and also anthropomorphic elements have found their way into Hebrew and Christian thought and practice at various times and places, and though modern theology and worship strives to eliminate all such elements the modern Christian will nevertheless not concede that his forerunners in the faith were entirely misguided. It will be insisted that their attitude was basically justified, but that what is essential had best be freed from all contamination from superstitious and anthropomorphic traces. Thus in so far as the Hebrews thought of the power of holiness as quasi-magical their views are rejected, and there is a general tendency to play down to the very minimum any terminology which depicts God as anthropomorphic. Modern Christian theology has made it clearer than ever how very extraordinary a person God must be, and it is with a view to doing as much justice as possible to this emphasis that I have developed my account of divine personality in terms of a perfect creative vision. In so far as superstitious and anthropomorphic elements have entered into

---

[1] See above p. 161-4. 　　　　[2] See above p. 247-74.

people's ideas about God the very meaning of holiness for them has been coloured accordingly, but where more sophisticated religious beliefs have been entertained that meaning has taken on a different hue. My task now is to consider what significance holiness will have for those who adopt the latter view and who regard their world as the expression of a perfect, creative vision. Let us reconsider in turn the points already raised in earlier chapters.

HOLINESS AND FEAR

The view I have put forward does not at all imply that the Holy One is not to be feared, but it does imply that he will not fall into the same category as the other objects of fear that we are acquainted with. On my view the fear of the holy is essentially the fear of a person, though the person in question is extraordinary. Does my account of this concept of an extraordinary 'person' throw any light on what is meant by 'fear of the holy' or 'fear of holiness'? In answering this question let us first consider the circumstances in which we would fear another human being.

Fear of another person would be an appropriate and justifiable reaction if, for instance, the person were in authority over us and we were uncertain as to whether he approved of our conduct. Our fear might express itself as an emotional disturbance when we are reminded of this person's presence and authority, or as a disposition to avoid doing anything which might displease him. This does not necessarily mean that we should be in constant fear and dread of that person, and indeed fear could give way to easy confidence whenever this person seemed to take kindly to us. A child's fear of his parents would be a good example, and one should note that the emotional aspect of fear may rarely be manifested in such a case even though fear in its dispositional aspect persists all along.

I would suggest that in the case of God, this 'authority' and 'approval' which is associated with fear and its removal should be understood in the light of the perfect creative vision. Any person's approval will depend upon his way of seeing things; God's approval will likewise depend upon his perfect vision.

Since the believer is not in a position to grasp this vision anything like adequately (though most believers would venture to claim that they know something of it through revelation) he will have less reason for complacency and every reason to think that his conduct could from the Holy One's point of view be improved upon. As regards authority, an ordinary person has it only to the extent of the power he has at his disposal. Anyone who can slip out of the grip of the power will have less reason to be afraid, but if the perfect vision is creative in the sense I have described then the power of the Holy One is without limit and there is no way of escape from it, for on it our very existence depends. Thus there will be no release from the fear of holiness except through coming to terms with the authority which gives rise to it.

Whenever persons, things, and places are taken as symbolizing or representing the Holy One they themselves are then likely to be treated as holy and the fear of the holy becomes associated with them. They are not objects of fear on their own account and if anyone takes them as such, attributing magical destructive powers to them perhaps, then the fear in question has become superstitious in character. To fear anything as holy is now seen as no less than to fear the extraordinary 'person' whom it bespeaks.

In so far as God is thought of as the one whose value-judgements are the absolute standard of goodness he would command respect rather than produce fear, but it would be an exceptional 'respect' far deeper than any that we have for the best of human persons, however wise and good they might be. The peculiarity of this 'respect' might be brought out in three stages beginning with the ordinary stage where one respects a person's demand because we see and judge his demand to be righteous and good by the standards of goodness which we ourselves accept. Secondly, we might think of a case where a person demands something of us and we do not quite see how the thing asked of us is righteous and good, but we believe that this person is in a better position than we are to make moral judgements. We might say, 'I don't quite see the virtue of doing this, but because it is *he* who asked me I shall do it, for I am sure that if I only had his depth of insight I should see the virtue of it as he apparently does.' The kind of respect we have for the person in this second case is different from, and in a sense profounder than, that of the first instance. But suppose there was a person making a demand upon us who is absolutely perfect in his moral righteousness, whose moral principles could never possibly be questioned, whose 'vision' is 'perfect' so that nothing is excluded, and whose value-judgements are final. Our regard for such a 'person' would be so profound that 'respect' is hardly the word for it. It would be 'veneration' or even 'adoration'.

It seems to me that if we understand fear of the holy in the light of a 'perfect vision' along the lines I have suggested, our discussion of it will have begun in the right direction. More needs to be said than is possible within the scope of this work, but I trust that the approach can be illuminating.

POWER AND HOLINESS

The understanding of holiness in terms of a 'perfect vision' also has implications for our understanding of the word 'power' when it is used in the religious context. If, to begin with, we consider power at the purely mechanical level we find that the term can be given a good empirical unpacking. A perfectly good mechanical explanation can be given of what we mean by the power of an engine, for instance. We should mention the effect of exploding a certain mixture within a cylinder in which a piston is fitted, and we should fill in the details of the story by referring to connecting rods, crankshaft, valves, sparking plugs, and so forth. At the mechanical level this explanation would be quite satisfactory; it would enable us to understand why one engine is more powerful than another, to build up new engines, to make use of combustion engines, and indeed at this level the meaning of 'power' would not worry us any more. This is what the word 'power' means when used of things as seen in the light of a mechanic's vision. On a similar plane we could have good accounts of electrical power from our electrical engineer, and even, for example, of muscular power from the biologist.

Suppose, however, we ask the mechanic why the fuel mixture of his engine explodes in the way it does, or why the cylinders of his engine keep their cylindrical form when under pressure. The enquiry would have shifted to a plane that was probably beyond him, yet of course there is sense in talking of power at this level too—the explosive power of the mixture, and the surrounding metal's power of resistance. We now know that such explanations could indeed be given, and we also know that if the mechanic's problem as well as that of the electrician and the biologist are taken far enough they all deposit their residue in the hands of the physicist. Furthermore, it is clearer today than it ever was how dependent we are upon 'insight' and 'vision' when enquiries are pursued this far.

The 'perfect vision' is not like the mechanic's vision or even the physicist's vision, but transcends all these. Since 'holiness', and therefore the 'power of holiness', is to be understood in terms of this 'perfect vision', it follows that it is not like any other ordinary power. This power is such that it could only be fully appreciated from the point of view of the 'perfect vision', and unless one reaches this level of insight or vision, holy power will remain mysterious despite all explanations that lesser insights might afford us. The 'perfect vision' is not ours, and therefore the holy power remains mysterious and beyond our comprehension, but that there *is* such a power has been suggested to various people in various circumstances. For some a blast of wind seems to have suggested it, for others a thunderstorm, and for some life-situations. As I said above,[3] Pedersen has shown clearly how the Hebrew worshipper associated life with the power of holiness which was regarded as its source. Again, Isaiah 41/17-20 expresses this by saying that the Holy One of Israel transformed the wilderness by bringing water into it, and planting in it 'the cedar, the acacia tree and the myrtle and the oil tree', and by setting in it 'the fir tree, the pine and the box tree together'. The immediate impact of such natural life-situations as these upon the prophet was to convince him of a powerful personal presence. There was no need to argue him *into* the conviction indeed it would be difficult to argue him out of it. When confronted by the present-day scientist with the incredibly complex, but co-ordinated, structure of the living cell the same prophet would no doubt have precisely the

[3] See page 62f.

same impression and conviction, and speak, expressing the ancient notion of 'wisdom' in a modern idiom, of the extraordinary power of the divine intellect. Not that he would necessarily regard the vision of such an intellect as merely commensurate with what he understood of the living cell, however fully he might understand it, but that the situation would suggest for him an intellect whose insight and vision so far surpasses his own as to be itself unsurpassable and perfect.

The concepts of the 'power of holiness' and of 'perfect vision' could be associated in another way as well. Consider the limited visions and correspondingly limited power which are displayed in the hierarchy of civil power. At a low level we have the local councillor with a vision and interest that is confined to local conditions, and who is able to exercise a corresponding measure of power. At a considerably higher level there is the cabinet minister who has to keep in view not just particular local problems but the general problems of all the localities in the country and whose power is correspondingly greater. At a higher level still the monarch in a monarchical state has, theoretically at any rate, to keep an eye on the whole complex life and order of his realm, and he is described in the old Bidding Prayer as someone who is 'over all persons and in all causes as well ecclesiastical as temporal within her dominions supreme' (supreme, that is, in power). But now think of the power of someone whose breadth of vision was all-extensive and excluded nothing; such, the Hebrew and Christian worshipper would claim, is the power of the Holy One. John Calvin bids us remember that the 'distribution of all the things which he (the Creator of heaven and earth) created are in his hand and power'.[4] We can imagine how much greater than ours is the power of a constitutional monarch whose oversight covers his whole realm. We cannot, indeed, imagine what the power of the overseer whose vision excludes nothing would be like, but we can sensibly suppose that there should be such a power, and such the power of holiness presumably is.

Again, if we think of the power of holiness as being a power of love, a reference to the 'perfect vision' should help us to

[4] *The Institutes of the Christian Religion* Vol. I p. 158.

understand what is involved here too. Let us consider an ordinary case of human love to begin with, that of a father who loves his child. There is nothing particularly puzzling about this kind of love and most of us believe we can understand it well enough. Most of us 'see' our own children as loveworthy creatures, and we are also fairly clear as to the sort of behaviour pattern that is an expression of love in such a case as this. But we can imagine cases in which we would be puzzled in both these respects. Sometimes we are puzzled as to how A can love B, for B seems so unlovable to us, and we may also be puzzled as to how a certain pattern of behaviour is an expression of love at all, for it seems unloving to us. However, it is possible in such cases for us to come to know B better, and to 'see' him or her as lovable after all. Also it may be possible to see A's pattern of behaviour in a new light, to 'see' what at first appeared to be inconsiderate behaviour as an expression of love. Such instances of love as this remain mysterious to us in so far as we fail to grasp A's vision of the total situation. We do not 'see' B as A sees him, and we do not understand A's be- haviour as A himself understands it. If and when we do acquire A's vision of the situation we may well estimate his love as being deeper and more far-reaching than other instances of what now appears to be rather more superficial love. But all this opens our eyes to further possibilities. May there not be a vision of people and the world which could be the source of a love that was beyond anything that we now understand? I have emphasized that the 'perfect vision' is beyond any and every possible vision, and that the love that is to be interpreted in the light of this vision would be exceptional indeed, very different from the love that is comprehensible to us, and to a large extent a mystery to us. Such, it seems to me, is divine love, or the 'love of God'. We should require to be in full pos- session of the 'perfect vision' ourselves if we were to appreciate such love properly, therefore we cannot fully explain what is meant by 'divine love', but it seems to me that a new line of discussion becomes possible when 'divine love' is understood in the light of the 'perfect vision'. The discussion of 'divine love' along these lines might, for instance, open up a fresh approach to some of the favourite themes of eighteenth century apologetic.[5]

HOLINESS AND SEPARATEDNESS

In this section I want to show how much better equipped we are to deal with a particular problem concerning holiness and separatedness if we think of the 'wholeness' which is holiness in terms of 'perfect vision'. It might be thought that if holiness implies separatedness, as often seems to be the case, then there is something which is separated from, and independent of, the 'divine whole'. Yet how can this be if the 'divine whole' is, as religious thinkers generally claim, all-embracing and infinite? We have already seen that one aspect of separatedness presents no insuperable difficulty, namely, the separation between the ordinary sphere of life and that which was kept inviolate as being holy. This becomes understandable when we realize that whatever was 'set apart' as being holy symbolized everything else that belonged to the ordinary sphere of life. For instance, in Hebrew religion the offering of the first-fruits to God in the sacrifice symbolized the fact that the whole harvest belonged to him. The problem arises when we consider another aspect of separatedness. We remember that the Hebrew set certain things apart, not as being holy, but because they were considered absolutely incompatible with holiness and capable of rendering other things unholy too if they were not kept quite separated. For instance, dead bodies were not to be touched; and, again, no one who committed adultery was tolerated in the tribal society. Are we to conclude then that there are some things which are intrinsically separated from the unity of holiness, and which therefore exist independently of that unity?

It seems to me that an interpretation of the unity of holiness in terms of the 'perfect vision' throws some light on our

[5] For example, Berkeley's treatment of the problem of evil in the *Principles of Human Knowledge* Part I sec. 153. He argues that if we 'enlarge our view', much that appears evil at first can be seen to be good. My suggestion would be that the religious believer must allow for, and have worshipful regard for, a view that is enlarged beyond anything we can ourselves imagine, a view enlarged to perfection. One could approach what Butler says in *The Analogy of Religion* Part I Ch. VII especially sec. 3 along the same lines and more sympathetically.

problem. The first implication of such an interpretation is, of course, that the unity of holiness is not at all like spatio-temporalunities, and that the separatedness implied in holiness is not spatio-temporal either. The word 'vision' suggests a very different kind of unity, and a correspondingly different kind of separatedness. To revert to an example already mentioned, consider the unity of a mechanic's vision of the world. The mechanic's eye concentrates on the mechanical aspect of every situation and ignores other features. Thus we can sensibly speak of such a thing as a mechanic's world, and this would have a certain unity which could only be understood in terms of the mechanic's vision. His vision may be said to separate out what is mechanical in a situation from that which is not. For instance, a mechanic as such would ignore such symbolic significance as a certain machine might have for an artist or a poet. Whatever the poet or artist may 'see' in the machine is 'separate' from what the mechanic sees, yet not in the sense of there being an extra bit which the mechanic cannot fit into his picture. So far as the mechanic *as such* is concerned that which the poet or artist sees is non-existent. In this case it is not that one part of the mechanic's world is separated from the next, but that what is separated from his world is non-existent so far as his vision is concerned. To be separated in such an example is to be non-existent, but of course what is non-existent for the mechanic is existent for others, such as the poet or the artist.

This gives us some hint as to what is meant by the unity implied in a 'perfect vision', and what is meant by separation from such a unity. Separation from this unity would imply non-existence so far as the 'perfect vision' is concerned. Furthermore, since this 'vision' is perfect, there could be no other vision in the light of which what is separate from it could be seen as existent. Therefore to be separate from the unity implied in the 'perfect vision' would involve absolute non-existence, and if separatedness from the 'divine whole' implies non-existence, then the problem with which we started does not arise any more.

It seems to me that such an account would be in harmony with the Biblical view of holiness. As I have already emphasized in an earlier chapter,[6] that which was to be kept quite separate from the holy was closely connected with diseases and death. We saw too that chaos and death were attributed to lack of harmony with the 'divine whole'. Again sin, which is alienation from God, is often represented as being 'death'. Death is naturally closely associated with the idea of non-existence, thus we see how our philosophical discussion links up with Biblical language.

ETHICS AND HOLINESS

We have seen how such theists as Otto, Oman and G. E. Hughes were concerned to emphasize that holiness implied a goodness which is more than ordinary moral goodness. We further saw that this emphasis upon an 'extra', which is 'more than' the morally good in the given sense of the term, could be satisfactorily allowed for, and the need for it explained, if there was an 'omniscient God' whose value-judgements are final and transcend all human value-judgements. Those conclusions can now be dovetailed into my account of God in terms of a 'perfect vision'.

Taking my cue from Hare, I have suggested that moral standards derive from fundamental decisions which constitute an expression of the person himself, decisions by which he 'makes himself', and furthermore that a person arrives at these decisions after taking into account the facts of the world around him as he understands them. In other words, the ultimate moral principles of a person depend upon his vision of the world around him, and his basic moral principles may be expected to alter or change in correspondence with the change in his vision. For example a parent A might in the light of his understanding of human nature commit himself to a certain basic principle as regards the upbringing of his children, but one of his children upon becoming himself a parent B, might modify the principle in the light of a different vision of human nature, a vision which was occasioned by a firm understanding of the advanced psychological explanations of his generation perhaps. Now, we can imagine a future parent C modifying still further this principle of child upbringing in the light of

[6] Chapter VII.

some superior vision of human nature. Similarly, other basic moral principles could change as man's vision of the world changes from age to age.

What of the moral principles that would be derived from a 'perfect vision'? They would be correspondingly superior to any that we know. We could not possibly appreciate them at our present stage of understanding any more than we know what the 'perfect vision' was like, although we should not expect them to contradict absolutely our present moral principles any more than the 'perfect vision' would be expected to make utter nonsense of, say, present-day scientific theories. But the point to emphasize here is that, just as 'perfect vision' is not to be identified with any particular vision that any human being now has, so also it would be quite wrong to identify the corresponding perfect morality with any set of moral principles at present held by any human beings. It follows from all this that the word 'good' would mean something very different if seen in the light of the 'perfect vision' from what the word means to us in our everyday language.

The word 'holy', when it qualifies the word 'goodness', could be understood as promoting the latter to such a logical status as to make it applicable to God. 'Holy goodness' would be a cumbersome term, and when people speak of the holy it is often the moral implication that is mainly in mind, thus we find that what should correctly be called 'holy goodness' is often simply called 'holiness', as though the word had none other than the moral implication. It should not be forgotten however that the word 'holy' has a wider reference than the moral one; its logical spread is best understood as I have suggested in terms of the 'perfect vision'. It is interesting to reflect on a parallel case to this viz. that of the word 'godliness'. This word is also generally used with the moral implication uppermost in mind, but again, 'godliness' might be expected to mean more than this in view of its derivation from the word 'God', and what people usually mean by 'godliness' might be more accurately termed 'godly goodness'. Still we cannot grudge the popular use of the shorter terms 'holiness' and 'godliness' to mean 'holy' or 'godly' goodness, so long as it is remembered that 'God' or 'holy' are not merely moral terms, and refer to

193

something more than the moral judgements of even a perfect being. They refer to the 'perfect vision', and indeed we have seen how we must refer to this 'perfect vision' in explaining what is meant by divine goodness.

Incidentally, this parallel between the logical behaviour of the words 'godliness' and 'holiness' lends further support to my contention that the terms 'God' and 'the holy' are in some contexts interchangeable. Both terms are especially associated with 'goodness' in the way I have just indicated, and they have the same effects when used as qualifiers with that word. This would be impossible if 'God' and 'holy' belonged to different logical frameworks and had different logical implications. Consider another example of the same sort of thing. The words 'physical' and 'mental' have very different implications, and this is clearly shown when the two words are used to qualify the one word 'blindness', for 'mental blindness' and 'physical blindness', are very different things. The terms 'intellectual blindness' and 'mental blindness' however indicate similar conditions, and the logical behaviour of the terms would be very similar—so similar in fact that it would hardly matter in most contexts which of the terms we used. All this indicates that the words 'mental' and 'intellectual' are logically very closely related, and that the situations in which their use is appropriate are very similar. The logical relationship between 'God', 'holy' and 'goodness' is comparable to this, and the upshot is that 'God' and 'holy' are logical kinsmen, which find an appropriate use in the same situations.

I come now to my general concluding remarks. One point which I hope has been made abundantly clear is that there is something quite extraordinary about the logic of the word 'holiness'—something which is shown by the special logical behaviour displayed by such terms as fear, power, and so forth, when they become closely associated with the word 'holy'. 'Holiness' does not belong to the same logical order as 'whiteness'; 'fear of the holy' is not of the same logical order as 'fear of the tiger' and 'holy power' is logically very different from 'horse power'. If we ignore this difference then we create unnecessary difficulties about religious language and blind ourselves to its true significance. To discuss 'holy power' on the assumption that this term is logically similar to 'horse power' will produce a confusion which is no less than what we get if we ignore the logical difference between the uses of the word 'factor' when we speak of prime 'factors' and of land 'factors' or, to take Professor Ryle's example, between 'honesty' and 'Mr Everest'.[7] The logical bankruptcy produced by discussing 'God' as though that word was logically similar to 'gardener', or even 'invisible gardener', is clearly brought out in A. G. N. Flew's article in *University* Number 1 (1950).[8] The religious believer has much to gain, and nothing to lose, by taking a lesson from contemporary philosophy on this point of distinguishing between the different logical behaviour of what may be grammatically similar words.

We should not look for holiness as an item amongst the observable features of the world, nor should we think of the concept of holiness as being verifiable in the same way as scientific concepts are. This needs to be emphasized for two reasons. In the first place, the critics of theism have too often tried to embarrass the religious believer by emphasizing that since his language is not about anything that is straightforwardly verifiable the supposed assertions made in that language are not assertions at all. This is, indeed, the sort of embarrassment that Flew tries to produce in the symposium to which I have just referred. It seems to me however that what we need is an account of the logic of assertions about holiness, an account which shows that such assertions are peculiar though not utterly and altogether so, and such an account is what I have attempted to provide. Secondly, religious believers themselves have been far too prone to look for a niche in the physical system into which they could fit a peg for hanging their religious beliefs. The result is what has been called a 'God of the gaps'. Anything that cannot be scientifically accounted for is sometimes offered as direct straightforward evidence for divine activity, but when the scientist succeeds in giving a satisfactory non-religious explanation for the piece of evidence in question another niche in the scientist's world must be found. What religious thinkers often fail to realize is that there are no

[7] See *Logic and Language* Series I Ch. II.
[8] Subsequently printed in *New Essays in Philosophical Theology* Ch. VI.

limits to the range of scientific explanation. It is far better, therefore, for the religious believer to realize and admit that religious language cannot compete with scientific language on its own ground. It has a very different kind of logic and the important task which confronts the present-day religious thinker is to make as clear as he can what kind of logic his language has, and the sort of topic it is trying to express.

There is no need to resort to forced interpretations, or to wide departure from religious discourse, in order to show the extraordinary logical status of religious language. Biblical and theological literature in general provides ample evidence of a remarkable awareness of the extraordinary nature of its subject, and drives us from all points into a realization that the logic of its language, in accordance with the nature of its subject, is extraordinary. It is not that we try to twist and stretch religious language so as to evade the thrusts of a challenging empiricist philosophy, but that religious language itself supersedes ordinary descriptive language since the latter is quite inadequate for the expression of religious awareness.

One must also try to avoid going into the opposite extreme of thinking that religious language is completely unrelated to ordinary discourse, and that its subject-matter is quite unrelated to our observable world. It seems to me that this is precisely what happens in Barthian theology. Barth himself in particular puts an extreme emphasis upon the oddness of religious language and knowledge. He goes as far as to say that 'knowledge of God is an antithesis to other knowledge'.[9] He rejects natural theology altogether in his attempt to isolate religious language and make it intelligible entirely from within.[10] It would seem on his view that no word can have true religious significance unless it is completely dissociated from all its connotations in ordinary discourse. For instance, he holds that Christian Monotheism has nothing at all to do with the ordinary meaning of the word 'one'—'nothing to do with the ordinary number "one" '.[11] It seems to me that this procedure

[9] *The Word of God and the Word of Man* p. 55 (Hodder & Stoughton, 1928).
[10] See *Natural Theology* (comprising Brunner's essay entitled 'Nature and Grace' and Barth's answer 'Nein') p. 76. (Centenary Press, 1946). It may be, however, that his view has undergone significant changes in recent years.
[11] *Dogmatics in Outline* p. 40 (S.C.M. Press, 1949).

makes things both too difficult and too easy. It makes religious language too difficult, and indeed impossible, for non-Barthians by cutting away all the lines of communication between ordinary discourse and theology; but it also makes religious language too easy by suggesting that there must be some secret direct access to its whole meaning independent of all other knowledge and understanding.

In my approach to the concept of holiness I have sought to avoid this extreme by showing that to understand what 'holiness' means we can, and must, begin with situations that are concrete and down to earth. Not that holiness is itself ever concrete or observable. Indeed, I have argued to the contrary. But it is always associated with concrete situations. For instance, we have seen how holiness has been thought of as a power and how, even though it was not ordinary power, it was also not experienced in complete isolation from ordinary powers either—the power of the thunder-storm, power of life, will-power and the power of love. Again, with regard to health and moral goodness, I have tried to make clear that though holiness meant *more* than all this, yet health and moral goodness were especially capable of harmonizing with the 'divine whole' with which 'holiness' would be associated. To say this is not to give to the question: what is holiness? an answer which will fully satisfy—if such an answer were ever possible. But it does give a starting point for possible discussion, especially with the non-believer. To seek such a point of engagement is all-important, except for those who seek no justification of religious belief and insist, for whatever diverse reasons, on asserting the unreasonableness of religion. As for those who try to combine scepticism with orthodoxy, they ought to be haunted by the ghost of Hume and thereby stirred to serious misgivings.

Certainly this discussion should be seen in contrast to any, and all, ventures of unreason, for it is precisely an attempt to show such reasonableness as religious discourse displays in one particular field. What I have tried to show is that, starting with the concept of holiness in all its contextual complexity, starting with discourse which includes talk about holy objects, fear, power, love, wholeness, separatedness, and morality, we can

eventually discern within this complexity some logical order—
an order which both suggests, and is illuminated by, the concept of a 'perfect vision'. Further, the usefulness of this concept
arises not least because of the logical links there are between
it and the concepts of 'personality' and 'God'. It is in this way
that the discussion is important, not so much for its final conclusions as for its methods and the suggestions thrown up on
the way. They are methods whose use implies that we never
finish learning, and it is indeed fitting that a book on the philosophy of religion should close on this note.

INDEX